God sure was good

John A. Walker

Printed by:
A&J Printing
P.O. Box 518
Nixa, MO 65714

Published by: J.A.W.'S Publishing

Order From:
Sgt. John A. Walker
530 Alger Ave.
Manistique, MI 49854
Phone: 906-341-2082
E-mail: jawspub@juno.com

Library of Congress Cataloging-In-Publication Data
Walker, John A.

ISBN 978-0-9639798-9-6

1st printing

Sgt. John A. Walker writes for:
Manistique Pioneer Tribune
212 Walnut St.
Manistique, MI 49854
Phone: 906-341-5200

These stories are written to show the humorous side of working as a Game Warden- living in Michigan's U.P. They are not meant to offend anyone and are just the writer's version of the stories as he heard or saw them happen. No names are used in the stories without prior approval.

A

I dedicate this book to these people as
representing so many that help me out with my books:

Mary Drier
Buck LeVasseur
Dave Richey

(Chapter 7)

Phil. 1-6

The U.P.
Upper Michigan

Lake Superior

Ontonagon

Area I Worked
District IV
Area 7

Canada

COPPER COUNTRY

Manistique

Lake Huron

Wisconsin

Lake Michigan

300 miles north of Milwaukee

Northern Michigan

300 Miles from Manistique to Lansing

Down State ⟶

Lansing(capital)

C

INDEX

A number of these stories, along with a number of the pictures, are out of the old Michigan Conservation Department archives.

D

Forewarned

Adapted from a newspaper article written by Mary Drier

Hunting stories abound, but books by a former Michigan game warden offer a different point of view from standard hunting tales.

Sgt. John A. Walker, a retired conservation officer, has nine books filled with a variety of hunting and other outdoor tales.

Some of the book's stories are from experiences when he was a game warden and some are stories he was told by other outdoor adventurers.

Walker recently completed his ninth self-published book entitled, *"Remember! Someone's Watching You!"*

"The idea for the books came about on the night I retired", said Walker.

"Some friends that attended my retirement party gave me a great gift. It was a hard, leather bound book written by a game warden from another state."

"It seems that everyone likes a good game warden story, even a retired game warden."

While the gift was a nice idea, Walker objected to the strong language used in the book.

"Friends and family members asked if they could read the book when I was done with it, but I wasn't half way through the first chapter when I knew that I wouldn't let anyone read that book," noted the former Michigan game warden.

"The language used ruined the whole book for me. I was not raised to talk that way, so, I decided there must be a need for a book that people of all ages could read without having to hide it from their kids or the kids hiding it from their parents, "said Walker.

E

"From the hundreds and hundreds of letters I've received and the more than 80,000 copies of my books I have sold, it appears there was a little niche for my type books."

His first book was titled, *A Deer Gets Revenge.* The others were published in the following order: *A Bucket of Bones; Land Where the Big Fish Live; Luck, Skill, Stupidity; Humans Are Nuts!; But Honey It Wasn't My Fault; Whatdaya Mean A Bad Attitude;* and *The Old School.*

All nine books contain humorous family-style backwoods short stories.

Walker began his career with the Conservation Department (later the DNR) in 1966 in Tuscola County, in Michigan's Thumb area, when he took a job as a fire officer.

In 1968 he became a game warden and stayed in Tuscola County for eight years before taking a promotion and transferring to Manistique in Michigan's Upper Peninsula in 1973.

"The stories are from the heart of an old game warden that had the greatest job in the world. In doing the job, I heard many great stories and had more fun living some of them than any one person should be allowed," said Walker

From his job as a game warden, Walker wrote fish reports for the Manistique Pioneer Tribune.

Some of the reports on hunting and fishing included some of the incidents from a game warden's life.

"The tales soon became more popular than the fish reporting," noted the author.

"I never in my wildest dreams ever thought the books from these Fish Report tales would go over like they have. Maybe I had a dream, but not enough faith."

Walker may have had little faith in his writing ability, but he does have plenty of faith.

For over 25 years he worked as a game warden and hunter safety instructor, and for 20 years he worked with teenagers from Bethel Baptist Church in Manistique.

"I made a promise to the Lord and myself that if any of my books sold I would place some money from each book sold through me into a scholarship fund to help youth from the church attend college," said Walker

As of 2006 his efforts have made it possible for more than 20 youth to receive some scholarship help with the start of each semester at college. To date more than $60,000 has been raised for the scholarship fund.

Walker has also traveled thousands of miles to tell his tales at banquets and outdoor shows. These story telling trips have taken him as far away as Alabama and Texas.

'It is my dream that I will, with the Lord's help, be able to have enough in the scholarship fund so the interest can accumulate and make it possible to hand out scholarships for years to come," Walker said.

Although a lot of the stories in the books relate to hunting, fishing, and growing up in the North Woods, Walker noted a successful adventure doesn't have to mean taking a trophy.

"If we are going to continue to enjoy hunting, fishing, plus enjoy the great outdoors, we had better get back to the times when 'success' does not decide whether we had a good time or not," said Walker.

"I may be in the minority of sportsmen, but I think we have lost the true love of hunting and fishing."

"I have written about it for years, and will keep on doing so till the day that I ride off to that perfect deer blind in the sky. Never will getting or catching something decide whether or not I had a good time in the woods."

"My dad taught me this point. I taught it to my kids and hunting buddies and I will tell it to anyone who will listen. Enjoy being alive and healthy, enjoy just being able to be out there and getting to be with family and friends. enjoy the camp time, and if the good Lord

G

should give you a 'bonus' and you are successful, just add it to the great time you had."

"Even if you do not hunt or fish, the great outdoors is there for all of us to share and enjoy."

"The most important thing you must remember is that whenever you go out into the outdoors whether it be hunting, fishing, hiking, or camping you are just building memories. You must also remember that the day will come faster than we want when all we will have left is the memories we have enjoyed with family and friends," Walker says.

"My dad told me years back that it seems that the older you get the faster the years seem to go by. This may be true and at my age I know it is, but it seems like you bring a new baby home from the hospital and before you know it they are off to college and striking out on their own," he says.

'So enjoy your spouse, the kids, and your friends while all of you are still able to build memories."

H

As the saying goes, "Everything and everybody reproduces something in life." So is it not just natural that hunters and fishermen should reproduce hunters and fishermen?

The picture of the boys on the cover of this book was taken during deer season at our hunting camp. (2006)

These are two of my grandsons walking down the road from camp to head out hunting with dad and grandpa.

People always ask what kind of deer season I had, which in the eyes of most people means, "Did you get a deer". I always tell them I had a great season because some of the kids got home and we got to spend time hunting with the grandkids. Needless to say this is our future if hunting and fishing is going to continue as we know it. It starts at or before the age of these two boys.

As you get older and the years seem to rush by remember all that you have at times when the kids are not around is the memories of time spent with them.

I think one of the greatest things I can recall is when some of the grandkids could either go to the Great America amusement park or spend time up north with grandma and grandpa and they chose to come to our house and go to camp.

As I say all the time, "Could life really get any better? "

I

Dear Friend,

I guess there is no way that I deserve all the blessings I have received in my life. God has been so good to me. I listened to my Dad while growing up and ended up with the job I always wanted since my high school days. While in the army I met and married my wife and God blessed us with four wonderful children. Now we have nine grandchildren. I could go on and on talking about the blessings of God, but there is something more important I would like to tell you about. While in the army a friend gave me a book titled The Greatest Story Ever Told. I read this book and it really got me thinking. Later I read the book called What Would Jesus do? From these two books I started to wonder about Jesus dying on the cross once for all and I realized that all included me. After meeting my wife I asked the Lord to forgive my sins and come into my heart, but there was always a little question in my heart about being saved. A couple of years later I attended some special meetings being preached by a bear hunting friend of mine Evangelist Pete Rice. During these meetings I made sure about my salvation and have never had this doubt in my heart again.

Once I heard Brother Pete preach on John 3:16 For God so loved the world that he gave his only begotten son, that whosoever believeth in Him should not perish, but have everlasting life. At the end of his preaching six people walked the isle to get saved. One was a tough, old, trapper that I knew and it really impressed me. What does being saved mean? It simply means that one understands that Jesus came and died on the cross for our sins, that we understand we are a sinner, and we ask Jesus to come into our heart, forgive our sins, and be our Savior.

You can use what is called the Romans Road to help you with this. It is as easy as driving down a 2-track out in the woods. If you would take a Bible you would find these verses. Romans 3:23 All have sinned and come short of the glory of God. This means that all people have sinned and need to realize it. Romans 6:23 states, the wages of sin is death. This means if we do not ask forgiveness of God for our sins we will die with payment due for them. I Corinthians 15:3 says, Christ died for our sins. This means payment has already been paid in full for our sins by Jesus death on the cross. Romans 6:23 tells us, the gift of God is eternal life through Jesus Christ our Lord. Everything that has to be done has been done, but for our part. Romans 10:13 tells us how, Whosoever shall call upon the name of the Lord shall be saved. This means all a person has to do is understand they are a sinner, that Jesus died on the cross for them, and ask Him to come into their heart and forgive their sins. Then you like so many before you will have ever lasting life to look forward to.

I pray you will do this and someday I will see you in heaven and you can tell me about it.

J

Wifee and Author

K

Baptist Church hosts annual Wild Game Dinner

Speaker at the Wild Game Dinner was Sgt. John Walker who is now retired from the Michigan Conservation Department. As a game warden in the Thumb and Upper Peninsula, he told many funny stories about his experiences with hunters who were legal and some who were illegal.

Picture Taken by Z Photography-Charles Zampich

L

Chapter 1
Conservation Officer's Stories **Upper Michigan Tales from a Game Warden's** **Perspective**
Are We Suppose to Love All God's Creatures

Working the job I had you were always confronted with those who had the job trying to convince the general public how wonderful and beneficial some creatures were. Here are a couple of tales that prove it can be a losing battle in the real world with women around.

Now Who's Batty?

Did you ever wonder just what may be the toughest job in the world to succeed in? I have come to the conclusion after much deep study just what jobs these are.

There is no doubt that the hardest job in the world is trying to convince people, especially women, what a wonderful asset to life snakes and bats are. Now I know they have tons of reasons why you should consider these two creatures part of the family if they happen to come and visit you, but I do wish you luck.

In fact, I have done a study twice this summer on the fact that having a bat come to visit you at night tends to upset the whole family. A while back we were up staying at camp with the grandkids, and Wifee (grandma) for some reason ended up on one of the top bunks. I had no sooner shut off the lights and got comfortable when the whole world came crashing down.

It seems Wifee's head no sooner hit the pillow than a bat decided to buzz between her head and the ceiling. You would not think grandma could get from the top bunk to the floor that quick, but there she stood and I knew what I had to look forward to.

Our guest on this night decided it may be better looking for lunch outside where there were not three hysterical girls running around.

Then would you believe the other night I woke up and heard something in the blinds in the bedroom window. There was no doubt what it was and I already knew just how Wifee would react. I chased it around for an hour and finally lost track of it somewhere in the house. We slept that night with the bedroom light on.

The next night all three of us had a good nights sleep, me, Wifee and the bat.

But the next evening as we were watching TV guess who dropped in? You're right, in swooped our batty friend right by wifee on the couch. When she finally recovered and settled back down on the floor she scared the bat on the front porch. We shut the door but this did not accomplish anything because he could not get outside from there.

So we blocked off all the outlets from the living room, opened the front door from the porch and let the bat back into the living room. As he came in I went out to the porch and opened the front outside door so he could leave the premises. There was only one problem. As we were doing this we lost sight of our guest.

We looked all over the room with no luck and finally figured he would return when he was ready. Wifee no sooner got settled back on the couch when he came from behind the couch right by Wifee's head. She was so impressed that she decided to jump up and down between our guest and the front door which rather defeated our game plan.

I explained to Wifee that our guest could hardly leave with her jumping around in the doorway. So no sooner did she move than our batty friend left the house and we could get back to normal hopefully for a long while.

Now the big question Wifee wants from me is to figure out how our guest got into the house in the first place. So I wish the person luck that has to change Wifee's mind about how wonderful having bats around are!

Batty Boy

One week in the Fish Report I talked about trying to teach ladies how wonderful bats are and how one should enjoy having them around. It must have hit a nerve because I received a number of phone calls and e-mails with stories about their experiences with bats.

One lady told about how one evening one decided to visit her at home. She said with the help of her husband she finally got it into the bathroom where it landed on the shower curtain. She quickly shut the door and got all ready to relax when all of a sudden she realized that everything in life was not perfect now. It all of a sudden dawned on her that she just may have to use the bathroom again in the future.

So she had to get up her nerve and enter the bathroom where she managed to catch the bat with a towel and get it outside.

Another story I got was this one.

Now I have to question who would be braver if it was a snake, not a bat. (This opening line is not fair because this person knows good and well how I feel about snakes.)

Last week on one of our stormy evenings, I was relaxing on the couch and reading the paper. Hubby had gone to bed a few minutes earlier. All of a sudden something flew by my paper and then it made a return visit right by the article that I was reading. Being the nice calm person that I am, It took a part of a second to assess the situation. Having assessed what was happening, I dodged the bat and went to get hubby out of bed. As you know he does not wear his processor (Her husband is deaf and has to wear this Processor in order to hear.) when sleeping.

So when I signaled him to get up, he thought the motion I made was a tornado warning for our area. He just doesn't get it, I also was pretty sharp, because when I went in the bedroom, so did our friendly bat. Again, the sharpness in me made a quick decision; I shut the bedroom door with hubby and the bat on the inside. I figured he would learn fast what the problem was. Wrong! He came out of the bedroom along with our new friend.

So while hubby is getting on his processor, our guest is making a tour of our house and I being my helpful self am getting the broom, for hubby naturally.

Our new guest must have been tired because it headed for the bedrooms. I did spot it going into the girl's room; I have good eyes for that type of thing. Now you have to realize, my other half is rather tired and not as fast as I think he should be.

3

After I can't find him (Batty Boy), he's not in here and a few more comments he finds Batty Boy (definitely a boy, because a girl would walk out when she is an unwelcome guest) on the curtain. He swatted at him, but he landed somewhere in the room. Now mind you I had just torn that room apart and super cleaned it, except for the bed, because I had birthday presents to wrap on the bed. Needless to say, I again tried to help by getting a flashlight so we could do a detailed search.

It seems our guest was investigating the presents, I suppose he thought they were for him. Whap! Another swat and the bat was ready for an outdoor vacation. Good thing I had those items on the bed, because an empty shoebox became his new outdoor home in the great outdoors.

Now I do not understand, with all the wonderful homes that are being built nowadays, why Batty Boy would want to visit two old folks like us.

Keep Trying

It is totally amazing but you can have people that have been to college or those that were lucky if they made it through high school and if you try to convince some of them of the benefits of having snakes and bats around you are wasting your breath.

If you should ever want to see a college graduate screech and run for cover get them out in the evening when the bats start swooping around the campground insect hunting. For some reason the old wives tale about bats getting tangled in your hair seems to outweigh the benefit of having them around. There is no way you are ever going to change some people's mind, but keep trying if you feel it is worth it.

Chapter 2

Conservation Officer's Stories
Upper Michigan Tales from a Game Warden's Perspective

Spent Bullets

I have told the story a number of times, of a lady getting hit by a shotgun slug that traveled all the way through her chest cavity from shoulder to shoulder, but did not hit any vital organs and after a trip to the emergency room went home. The doctor said that there was no way something like this could happen in a million tries, but it did.

What an Obituary this Would Have Made

Besides if you think you have had a strange day think of this guy.

A man was sitting on the toilet in his hunting camp when all of a sudden the top of the toilet tank just seemed to explode. The man looked to his left and saw a bullet hole in his shower stall. He looked the other way and saw where the bullet had ricocheted off the wall into the tank top.

The man and his hunting buddies ran outside and saw another hunter standing out in a field about 50 yards from their camp. They yelled at the man who yelled back that he had just shot at a deer and missed. This hunter then walked away, going off into the woods.

At this point the man who had been sitting on the toilet at the time of the shot noticed where the bullet had passed into and through the right leg of his pants. A game warden was called who tracked the shooter down and issued him a ticket for reckless use of a firearm.

Nine Lives?

With all the time I have spent in the woods through the years there are still times when you hear a shot go off real close to you it makes you wonder just what the shooter is shooting at. This story is rather scary when you stop and think about it

....

5

In the travels with my books earlier this month I ran into a party that told me a rather interesting tale. He had a couple of my books already and came over to purchase the ones he was missing. As we were talking he said, "My long vacation is over because the doctor told me I could go back to work Monday."

He then told me that he had been riding his 4-wheeler back two months ago without a care in the world. That was until he came around a corner and a party that was target practicing with a high powered rifle without any kind of a backstop shot him through the stomach.

He said, "I guess it just wasn't my time, because everything fell into place and they got me to the hospital in time."

But it had taken him two months to get fully back on his feet.

The bottom line to this story is that you never know who else may be running around out in the woods when you think you are the only person for miles around. In other words playing and doing things safely should just be done automatically.

Do You Hear Something?

Did you ever stop and think that God must have a weird sense of humor? It has always amazed me how a nice bright green fern can dry up and turn brown in the fall and then take on the perfect shape of a pat standing on the edge of the woods. Or how many times have you spotted this bird, took a step back to check it out, moved a little closer as you got ready for it to flush, only to realize it is a piece of a tree root.

This root looks more like a pat than some of the carvings you see at outdoor shows. Of course what really gets you is when you finally figure out what it is, only to have it flush when you have your gun down. There are always days out in the woods when you figure life is not really being fair to you.

This and the fact that a half dozen times this year when going through some heavy cover trying to put up a pat I have been attacked by mad rabbits taking off from right under my feet! I am not hunting rabbits so I watch as he takes off and tries to hide his half white body in the brown cover. All the time I'm wondering if I should just invite him to dinner, and make him the guest of honor, for scaring the fire out of me. I have put up a dozen or more rabbits this fall. This is the most I have seen in a good number of years.

Then there is the case where you had better beware that cold weather could get you into trouble.

You could say that not all those out in the woods are the brightest bulb on the block, but I won't. Or you could say that cold weather is not always what it is cracked up to be.

It seems that there was this crew of deer hunters out beating the brush trying to get a deer. They had all come out together in one of the guy's work van. As they worked their way back to the van for lunch one of our hunters spied a rather large bee's nest up in a tree. He figured it would be perfect for his grandson to take to school for show and tell so he shot the nest out of the tree, and threw it in the van, to take home.

This crew went back out hunting and later returned to the van to head home. As they were driving back to the house, and they had a good ways to go, they turned on the heat in the van to warm up. A short time later they all of a sudden realized there were more bodies inside the van than there were members of the hunting party. They managed to swat the first couple only to suddenly realize they were greatly outnumbered. The van came to a sliding stop on the edge of the road as drastic action had to be taken.

It seems as the van got good and warm the hunters were not the only thing that came to life from all the heat so did all the bee's in the nest laying in the back of the van. This crew was lucky enough that there was a can of starter fluid in the van that worked good on convincing all the bee's inside and outside the nest to go back to sleep.

So be careful out there you may end up with more than you bargain for.

7

Where you went on a date in the U.P. when I was growing up. It was small town U.P. nightly activity for the whole family

Chapter 3

Conservation Officer's Stories
Upper Michigan Tales from a Game Warden's Perspective

Modern Technology

A Picture is Worth a Thousand Words

In reading through and hearing some stories of this past hunting season one has to wonder what some hunters are thinking. You hear all the time about hunters hunting over lighted bait piles, not wearing hunters orange, or felony with a firearm. The last one is being enforced a lot more after 9/11. As I read over and over how some hunters will go to any extent to get a deer I have to wonder where their other priorities are in life?

Then there are those that have yet to figure out that you cannot outwit a computer as to if and when you purchased a license. But you would not believe how many people still try. "I just forgot to get my new license." When a computer check soon shows the party had never purchased a license in his life.

Or the fact that there are those (and a lot more than you may think) out there that have the capability of taking a picture or even a short movie with their cell phone as to the violations they see. It has to be rather interesting when a poacher finds out he has become a movie star back in the middle of no-where where he thought he was the only person on the planet.

There was a case where this was used in calling in a poaching violation where not only did the game warden receive a phone call but some pictures came through at the same time showing the violation taking place.

Things are changing and a lot faster than some of us old fossils can comprehend.

In fact, I was speaking at a banquet one night when I mentioned that it is almost impossible for a party to get lost out in the woods anymore in this day and age.

I stated that all the party would have to do when he could not figure out where he was and how to get back out is to call his wife on his cell phone and she would come and get him.

About this time a voice from the back of the room yelled, 'I would rather stay lost than call the wife and admit I was lost!"

Buddies?

Some buddies are better off not being your buddies.

I heard from a man this past week that had been out hunting last year and shot a pat for the first time in years. His buddy with him built him up on his expertise so when he got home they took a picture of his "partridge" and sent it off to his buddies with a message saying you should have been here.

It seems that one of his buddies, using the word loosely, that received the picture of the "partridge" figured he would forward it to the DNR.

About two days later our successful partridge hunter heard a knock on his door and the local Conservation Officer was there to talk to him about the picture he had of his "partridge".

Our successful hunter was informed it was not a pat after all but a Spruce Hen! He told me the worst part of it was his "buddies" knew all the time what it was and never told him so his lesson in life cost him $150.00. What made it even more interesting he was laughing about it and the fact they had stuck him good.

It makes one wonder just what kind of "buddies" this group of hunters are and what goes on between them to get back at each other.

Stumped Again

You know one thing that has always amazed me is where fishermen claim to love the sport and enjoy just being able to get out on the water and do a little fishing. They use it for a break from the pressure cooker they are in all week.

I have to ask if they love the sport and enjoy it so much, how come you read so often where they do not care enough about it to be thankful when they limit out and call it a day? How come so many of them will run their limit of walleye back to the cabin and head out again to see if they can limit out again? When you realize what a small percentage of poachers ever get caught how many fish are actually taken over the limit?

Just multiply what I heard about in one week and what would be the real total? There was a party caught with 50 blue gills over his limit. There was another party that had 34 brook trout and of these 19 were undersize. There was another party that had 15 walleye over the legal limit.

While still another party had 14 undersize walleye in his possession. I have to wonder how much complaining these same fishermen would do if the fishing seemed to drop off where they fished.

Of course there may be those doing something wrong that even the game warden cannot do anything about.

One day while out on patrol I came to an area where there was a small creek that ran into a bay area. As I pulled into this area that was popular for people fishing both out in a boat and from shore I decided to walk down to the mouth of the creek and see if anyone was fishing there.

As I came within sight of the bay area I saw two couples fishing. The men were out in the bay with waders and the ladies were fishing the creek mouth from the bank. As I walked towards them, and it was a good distance, the ladies saw me coming.

Now one of the ladies was rather large, or should I say really large. As I walked towards them I saw her pick up a couple of what appeared to be fish lying on the bank and drop them down the front of her blouse. Bass season was not open and this was a good area for fishing for bass.

I walked up and the men walked into shore and I checked all their fishing license. The one lady managed to show me her license without ever leaving her sitting position. Now I was sure there was a violation here, but Mrs. Walker did not raise any dummy, so I figured about all I could do was talk with the people for a while as she had to sit there with those slimy fish down her blouse on this hot summer day.

11

The thought did pass through my mind to ask her to stand up and do a few jumping jacks, but after seeing how big she was I figured to pass on this one.

So once in a while even the game warden comes to those no win situations.

Perfect Landing

Did you hear about the wife that wanted to go hunting with hubby? So he went out and got her a bow and all the equipment so she could get some practice in before bow season opened. Then he went and got her a tree stand so she would have a place to hunt. He set this stand up just far enough away from him so she could find him if anything happened. They now were all ready for when bow season opened.

They headed out opening day and he first stopped at her tree stand and watched her get up in it, all set for her first hunt. Then he headed over the ridge to his tree stand.

Just a short time later he heard something busting through the brush and a loud thud between his stand and his wife's. He waited for something to come past him but nothing did. Then it was all quiet.

He sat for an hour and a half or more and then decided to walk over to his wife's stand and see if she was ready to head out. As he came to where he could see her stand he noticed that she was no longer sitting up in the tree.

He continued on and when he got through the brush under her stand he soon knew why! There she lay on the ground at the bottom of the tree out like a light. It seems she had tried to adjust her safety harness when all of a sudden she realized she was now airborne. She landed in the brush at the bottom of the tree and was not hurt but had been knocked out. But then she lay there for an hour and a half too scared to move for fear she was hurt waiting for her husband to come by.

She figured he should be right there because there was no way he could miss hearing all the brush breaking and the thud when she hit the ground. Of course he had heard it but figured it was something going off through the woods not his wife flying through the air and crashing into the ground.

Now he has a little used tree stand and bow for sale because his wife got all the desire to hunt knocked out of her when she hit the ground.

Flying Turkey Dinner

Do you realize that a number of our forefathers wanted to make the turkey our national bird? I am not kidding! There were those that felt that the Eastern wild turkey should be our national bird because of it's beauty, durability, and how smart they are in outwitting a hunter.

Of course if this had happened, they would more than likely be protected and we would be having eagle for Thanksgiving dinner. When you stop and think about it maybe we did luck out the way things turned out after all.

Speaking of turkey season, did you hear about the guy that managed to bag a nice tom? He placed it in the trunk of his car and headed home. On the way he stopped to show some of his buddies his trophy bird. He told them what a magnificent bird he had managed to bag and the whole story about how he had outwitted this bird. Of course he had to show off his bird so they went to the back of his car so he could show them his trophy.

He reached over and unlocked the trunk and as the lid flew open out flew his trophy tom turkey wings just a flapping. The hunter and his buddies ducked out of the way as he got airborne and flew off into the wild blue yonder as they all stood there in shock! So if you should bag a nice tom turkey with a kill tag on it already you will be the last chapter in this hunting adventure.

Vintage hunting camps

Chapter 4

Conservation Officer's Stories
Upper Michigan Tales from a Game Warden's Perspective

Times Are "A" Changing

A few times in my weekly article I have written stories that tell just why some of the attitudes towards the DNR may have changed over the last few years. One week I wrote about changes in the licensing system that was suppose to set the DNR budget on a steady course. Now let me tell you about some other changes I have watched take place.

The Real Criminals

First of all I want to point out there are always two-sides to every story.

When I was growing up every kid in the backwoods spent time outdoors doing things that were really not legal under the letter of the law, but it was a way of life up here in Michigan's U.P.

In the spring you would go down to the creek where the suckers ran and dam up the creek then make your own spears out of a tag alder to try to spear some suckers.

More times than not your project ended up being a wet and muddy mess with very few suckers to show for it.

During the winter you would see where at least a zillion rabbits were moving around at night so you and your buddies would come up with some ingenious ways of trying to trap or catch rabbits. We never did catch any, but it was not for the lack of trying.

When I was working it stated in the law that you needed a hunting license for slingshots, along with some pellet guns, but we never really went out of our way worrying about this fact. Now I have been told where dad's have been told that their little hunting buddy cannot carry his BB gun without a hunting license when out with dad. If this be the case, is there not maybe a reason hunters numbers are going down?

Then there was the case where a youth, not yet a teenager, figured out a way to make a little money during the summer. Instead of setting up a kool-aid stand he got an old wash tub and caught a few minnows from the creek next to the barn and tried to sell a few minnows. Would you believe the next thing he knew he was talking to a Conservation Officer about the fact that what he was doing was illegal and you needed a license to sell minnows? Are you not sometimes better off using a little wisdom in what you see and don't see out there?

Then there was the dad that was going to take the kids out fishing. Seeing it was a nice sunny day mom decided to go along and get in a little sun bathing while dad and the kids were fishing. They had a nice enough boat so she could spread out a blanket and soak up the sun while the others fished. Along comes a Conservation Officer to check out those fishing. When it is observed that there are four people and four poles she insists that mom needs a license if she was fishing. They did not ask if she was fishing, but took the fact that there was a pole for each body that she was. A bad taste was left with this family even though a ticket was not issued.

I will close with this fact that you may find hard to believe with the way things are done today. Please remember the way the law is written has not changed. The department policy book stated that the only time you could write a party a ticket for having an uncased gun in a motor vehicle was if there was an overt act of hunting. This meant that the gun was sticking out the window being aimed at something.

You see times have changed; interpretations of the same laws have changed, and the way things are looked at by those enforcing the laws have changed. One does not have to wonder why the numbers are going down and not one legislator wants to go out on a limb for today's DNR.

Grandma's Bear

I was told this story first by the husband and later his wife showed me the pictures and retold the story and would you believe it both told the same story.

Both of these two hunters are retired and have spent time hunting from Michigan to Texas with even some side trips to hunt in Africa.

16

This past year they had hunted successfully in both Michigan and Texas.

It seems that the wife had drawn a successful bear permit to hunt the Drummond Island area. Seeing she had the permit her husband had to be the official bear guide. But they had always hunted together so this was not really a problem for either of them.

They made their plans to head up to Drummond Island for the hunt and she must have had an excellent guide for she managed to score with a trophy size black bear that weighed in at more than 450 pounds. Needless to say a lot of pictures were taken.

They returned home with their prize black bear and decided to have a full mount made of the wife's bear standing up. They already had a trophy room at the house with mounts from their hunts at home and around the world.

Everything was going along great when they found some speed bumps in the road. It seems that the local game warden had been at the taxidermist shop checking on some things when the owner of the shop happened to mention who had shot the large black bear mount he was working on.

When the taxidermist told the officer that a 75 year old woman had shot the bear the officer right away figured there was no way a lady this old shot this large 475 pound bear.

With nothing to go on, it seems the local officer went to the home of this older couple and with no tact at all, accused the older lady and her husband of the fact this 75 year little old lady could not have killed this bear!

Needless to say the husband that is a little fire ball of a guy was not a happy camper when this officer accused his wife of violating and she could not have shot this bear.

The husband tried to solve this problem as best he could without really blowing his stack so he suggested, "See down the driveway there my mailbox is just about 150 yards down the hill. Now you go down there and line up by the mail box and if my wife cannot drop you before you can run half way across the driveway at 150 yards distance with her bear rifle, you can come back and write her a ticket for poaching her bear and we will pay the fine without another word."

The officer figured just maybe this guy was half way serious and just maybe his 75 year old wife had been capable of shooting this bear after all.

The man of the house suggested the officer leave his property before he really got upset.

Brain Dead?

One week in the Fish Report I wanted to revisit something I have talked about before. As a lot of you know I attend a number of shows in the fall of the year with my books. In the areas where I go I get to see a good number of DNR employees that I worked with. We usually spend time talking about how things are and used to be.

There is a reason that so many "Exspurts" have wanted history dropped from being taught in school. There is also a reason why our nation has always been able to handle any type challenge that came their way.

Most of us from the "Old School" were taught to think! We were taught to look situations over and handle them as we felt they should be handled based on the circumstances involved with each situation. It was instilled in each person that they could handle whatever came their way by applying the training they had and they were able to check out the facts and apply them. But folks I have to tell you things have changed.

You hear over and over horror stories about how the local conservation officer seemed to handle a situation. First of all let me say right off that sometimes we do not hear the complete story from both sides. But now there seems to be another overriding factor dictating what should takes place. I have heard from a good number of both present and former DNR employees that, "You would not believe how bad it really is." "We are no longer allowed to think for ourselves.

But let me say I have also heard this same statement from employees of other law enforcement agencies. It almost seems like this has become a national trend that is now being pushed by

18

the powers in being at the "Big House." They do not seem to want an officer to use his brain and common sense anymore. They seem to want everything in life to be handled in a black and white world. Or one size fits all. In a real world life it does not work this way, because a lot of times different circumstances surround each case.

It seems that the day when officers were sent out to check out a report on something they were expected to handle the case the way the circumstances justified. In other words after the facts were collected action was taken based on the facts of this individual case. When this was done usually the action taken was fair on both sides. Not that both sides always agreed on the action taken, but they understood why this action was taken.

There seems to be a push by those in the "Big House" to have "mind controlled robots" out in the field enforcing our laws rather than hiring good people that are capable of checking out what took place, using their brain and good common sense, and taking appropriate action. Let me say from what I hear this is not the fault of people in the field but handed down from those running the departments without any flexibility on the officer's part.

Now don't get me wrong any business or department, especially a law enforcement agency, has to have policy and training in how the job they are doing should be done. You cannot have a 250 officer department going off in 250 different directions. But I think every situation can be different and should be looked at as to what just took place.

I will put it in simple terms so you can maybe see what I am getting at. Where I used to have fun with my boss up at Newberry, I always told him some Sunday morning I was going out on patrol up in Newberry along the highway. I was going to sit between town and the golf course. You see right along the edge of the road running from town out to the golf course was this little trail where all those that went golfing rode their golf carts from town to the golf course a mile or more away. Under the letter of the ORV laws, and it was a black and white ORV violation to do this seeing a golf cart is for sure an off-road vehicle. And none of them had a valid ORV sticker on their carts.

When I told him what I was going to do in so many words he threatened me with my life if I should even think about sitting out there. Back in those days I guess you could also do this or at least threaten to afflict great bodily harm upon one if you felt it was a dumb idea.

So as you get ready to hit the woods this fall just remember to go over the law digest and remember that the "Old School" days are a thing of history in today's world.

....

I know that everybody has their version of a story or what really happened out there when they were checked by the local game warden, but if just a percentage of all the stories I have been told are true it is too many.

I always tell this story of how I was trained to treat people right. My boss at the time had been a Detroit police officer before becoming a conservation officer. He taught me that if you were checking a man out hunting with his son, and you found a minor violation you were to treat it as such. He told me that the proper way to handle the situation was to take the father aside and tell him what you could do and a ticket could be issued. Then tell them that you are not going to issue a ticket because you do not want to embarrass dad in front of his sons.

He told me the father-son relationship and the fact they were out enjoying the outdoors together was more important than issuing a ticket.

Was he right, who can say, but it was the way I was taught.

Chapter 5

Conservation Officer's Stories
Upper Michigan Tales from a Game Warden's Perspective

My Opinion

There is a real reason that most outdoor adventures such as a game warden have a dog that tags along with them. It is apparent if you remember that after all the long hours spent out there by themselves, they have to have someone to discuss all the world problems with.

One good thing about holding a conversation with your dog is that he never talks back, they never have a different opinion than what you are telling them. Of course they may look at you at times with that look of wonderment in their eyes, but they will soon realize who feeds them so they will let it pass.

Here are a few such opinions that I have run by my dog.

Global Warming

In one of my newspaper articles I talked about the fact that you could melt snow with the sun shining in cold weather and I guess this week has really proved my point. Can you imagine how cold it would have felt if it had not been for the sunshine we had during this cold snap? For the life of me I cannot figure out how some people can figure this system of ours was all just an accident. If you stop and think about it there is no way everything that takes place could just happen by chance.

Seeing most of us are trying to find ways to stay warm with the weather we have had I thought I would give you something to warm you up as you think on it. In fact for some people it may reach the boiling point.

It totally amazes me how things have turned around in my lifetime. People will read an article on something and never even stop and think about what it really says. In fact I think most people read the headline and to them that is the whole article.

I read a headline this week that sure falls into this category. It read "Humans cause global warming". Now I am sure one has to have at least fifty years of college to come up with a headline like this.

First you have to remember that 90% of these scientists that have this opinion do not believe in the God some of us believe created this earth, so they are left with only one other place to throw the blame. There are not really too many directions to throw the blame but at us humans.

From someone who has spent their whole life in the great outdoors and has been rubbing elbows with those in the environmental field for years one has to wonder. I have stated in the Fish Report time and time again that one of the things that really bothers me is when someone has the "official" approved opinion, but when you get a chance to sit and talk with them one on one, they will confide in you a whole different story. They just cannot give their opinion when it differs with the "official" opinion.

How many of you can remember not so many years back when we had a period of real cold winters that the official word was that the "ice age" was going to return and glaciers would once again start working their way south from the North Pole?

Or we will have a couple of real dry seasons and a ten year drought is descending upon us. This only to be proven wrong when we have monsoons for the next three years in a row. How come scientists can throw out all these earth ending theories only to be proven wrong by nature and not have to answer for their actions. It kind of reminds me of some politicians that can state a fact as gospel only to find out later there was no truth to it and they are never made to answer for their comments.

I just have to wonder when we "humans" cannot report the weather accurately for a ten day period, how can we say, "In the year 2079 there is going to be a real problem with the weather patterns." So as you read the "official" scary opinion make sure to look into and read the whole article and also read a selection of articles on the subject. One truth you can believe in is that there is a reason history is not being studied and taught any more.

Of course speaking of our weather I will take it any day over what they have had in some other parts of the country. Snow and cold you can always get ready for, but ice and tornados are all together different.

I will close with the following that reminds some of us old fossils that there were times we could have used a little Global warming.

The Little Building Way Out Back: Here's a little information, That perhaps you'd like to know, About the outdoor plumbing, That we had so many years ago.

Not approved by city folks, But farm folks (and Yoopers) can recall, When those little Privies, Weren't considered bad at all.

Most of those little sheds, Were fashioned with two holes, For paper, dated catalogs, It didn't come in rolls.

How we recall those catalogs, We used 'em up real fast, Especially those thin pages, The glossy ones were last.

We always bought from SEARS, Our parents weren't so dumb, And everyone was happy, When new catalogs would come.

Those were handy buildings, But we never tho't 'twas right, When nature made a call In the middle of a winter night!

Sometimes it would happen, And all you'd really need, To avoid some frozen complications, was a little extra speed.

But my, how things have changed, We view the change with pride, Now we eat outdoors, And the bathroom is inside!

We don't miss those old days, Tho, we did have lots of fun, But we still are mighty glad, That those "Good Old Days" are done!

DNR Budget Solutions

In another one of my articles I have written a little about the case for a license increase with the number of hunters and fishermen going down each year. I also stated that I would follow up with a few facts that I think gives people this attitude.

First of all let me mention one that hits right here at home. Through the years the DNR has closed more and more of their field offices so that people feel they are cut off from the DNR. We had one closed at the Thompson Hatchery that was closed more for political reasons than anything else. I could go across the U.P. and name field office after field office that has been closed and the interesting thing is that in a lot of cases the personnel that you could catch at one of these field offices are still working but no longer around to stop and talk too. You have to remember that not everyone has a computer to look things up so they just feel left out.

When these field offices were closed it caused another contact to be lost. Now I will admit this one could be a real pain for the officers or those at the field office, but it was a service to the public. Do you remember when if you had a skunk or woodchuck problem you could go to the field office and check out a live trap? Or if it was a little old lady having a problem we even went and trapped the critters for her. Not in this day and age, it is just another service lost.

Also when the field offices closed the successful hunters lost a place where they could go and get their successful hunters patch. Now in some cases here in the U.P. you have to drive over 100 miles round trip to get a patch. Just another service lost to the outdoor public.

Okay you old fossils out there I need some help with the year this actually happened. Do you remember when if the husband bought a fishing license it became a family outing because your wife did not have to purchase a fishing license? Then the "Exspurts" decided that they could solve all the budget problems if they changed the law so mom also had to purchase a fishing license. Now if this was true we really should have doubled the number of fishing licenses sold. (Not really) But there should have been a sharp increase in the number of license sold. But was the price we paid when mom could no longer fish free on dad's license worth it for the next generation of youth to grow up without family fishing trips. Just food for thought.

Then they were going to solve all the financial problems by making those that fish in the great lakes buy a fishing license. This was also done to help with the Salmon program so there was a plus for the fishermen, but it did not solve the problem.

I even remember when snowmachines did not need a license and now they need two. So the outdoor person has to purchase two snowmobile license, an ORV license, and a boat license. Now through the year's boat license have went from only those that used a motor needing a registration, to now where almost all type of watercraft need a license.

I just wanted to point some of these things out that through the years were used to fix the DNR's budget problems and they never did. Now like any business when they get a big influx of cash they can survive a number of years living on the cash flow from the increase. There are a lot of private businesses that try to do this when they first get started and they soon find out they have to change or in a couple of years their doors will be closed.

What usually happens with government is when they get an increase and an influx of cash they start creating new programs, which means new personnel, which means your new cash flow is eaten up in a short time.

I will use this to prove my point. When I hired in as a Conservation Officer there were four people in the Lansing DNR law section. The chief of law division, his assistant and a secretary. There was also one person in the Hunter Safety section. When I left 25 years later there was ten times that many in the Lansing office with even fewer field Conservation Officers. AND remember this was just one department within the DNR so money problems should be no surprise. Now we will talk about how attitudes have also changed.

Easy To Understand, Right

I am going to try and explain a couple of things in this article that I have had questions on. I might add that I also get more questions on this subject than anything else.

First let's talk about ORV's or as for some dumb reason the Federal Government now calls OHV's. To most of us they are one and the same.

Let me say right off that before the ink is dry on this article things could change because there has to be a full time crew in government working on changes 24-7.

What I was told is that if a road or 2-track has a numbered sign post on it you have to look at the way the numbers run. If the letters are up and down or vertical this trail is open to ORV traffic.

If the road or 2-track has a sign where the numbers run horizontal or left to right this trail is closed to ORV traffic. This is usually the better developed roads out there.

But! Needless to say there is even an exception to this way of figuring out where you can or cannot ride. This is where there is either a sign on the numbered post with an ORV on it showing you either can or cannot operate on this road.

I was told that one of the keys is that there has to be a numbered sign on the road for it to be considered either opened or closed. In other words the old skid roads, trails that follow ridges back into the backwoods, or any other ORV trails that are not posted or numbered are not legal trails.

Another thing that is not clear in the hunting guide is where it says you can use an ORV to retrieve legally taken deer. (Notice it says legally taken deer in the guide.) The way this is worded can get you in trouble because the U.S. Forest Service does not allow this on their forest land. Therefore when it says this it applies to state and corporation lands only.

Now have you got this all figured out? This is the best I can tell you from what was told to me.

The other thing that has come up is where you see trees throughout the forest that have been girdled with a tag hanging on them. A short time later you will see this tree cut up and parts removed. There is one in the opening just before you get to the National Forests.

Like a lot of you I was trying to figure out what was going on and happened to see someone I could ask. It seems this is a study for the Ash bore that has infected Michigan. It seems there is a crew going throughout the forest doing a study on Ash trees to see if it has moved into our area.

So now you know as much as I do about what is going on with these two items. Hopefully it will help keep you out of trouble or should I say, hopefully it will until the next change comes along.

You know being raised like I was and having a job where you were paid by the tax payers all my life, maybe I look at things a little different than most people. I have run into a number of things during the last hunting season that really makes one wonder just where we are going in this country.

Years ago I purchased a nice stainless steel 22 rifle with a nylon stock for a gift for someone. It was made and manufactured by one of the two biggest named gun companies at the time. I looked at the same firearm a while back, the same model, with all the same markings; you would have to work to find anything to tell these two rifles apart. That is all but one little item where it now said, "Made in Brazil". I could not believe it.

Now take the time to look around as you shop and you will see where it seems like everything you purchase now is "Made in China". Not just a few things but everywhere you shop and so many things you buy now.

As I have already said before, La Crosse boots made in China! No wonder they don't teach geography in school anymore. I always thought La Crosse was in Wisconsin but now even that has moved to China. It is rather scary when you stop and think about what is taking place.

Do you remember when the big boy now Wal-Mart built it's reputation on "Made in America"? There were signs all over their store bragging about this fact until someone read the labels on enough of the products sold there and they were made to take the signs down. Look around in there now and see how many items in their store are "Home Made" so to speak.

Here's a history lesson for all you up here that were born after the "Big War". I can remember back in the 50's, this is back in the middle of the last century that we wanted to buy one of those new gadgets called a transistor radio for my Dad for his birthday so he could use it up at camp. My Dad was a member of the union at the paper mill and he always told us kids, "Buy made in USA, because we can't compete with Japan where they hire people for twenty-five cents an hour to do what we do here"! So we looked all over the area until we found a Channel Master radio that had "Made in

USA" on it to get for Dad. It was the only one we could find out of all of those that were out there.

Food for thought at the start of 2004, was not my Dad way before his time in teaching his children about what was to come in the future? It totally amazed me when I saw where so much of the hunting and fishing items purchased in this country are made in nations that if you stop and think about it have no use for the "Good Old USA". I'm sorry but this bothers this red blooded, flag waving, Yooper.

Federal Evolution

Do you realize that it was accepted as fact that states had the rights to control fish and wildlife within their borders for more than a century in our nation? Then thanks to some of the rulings pushed through to set regulations trapping right up here in the U.P., the federal government for one of the first times in the history usurped their authority on a state to set hunting and trapping rights. This was one of the first steps in a long downward slide where a Federal Judge out in a far western state can set rules for what can and cannot be done in Michigan. It is another prime example of where local and state government can lose their day in what happens within their borders.

It was always a fact that the federal government had a hand in setting rules for hunting migratory birds because of the fact they crossed state and even national borders. But it was not always law where the federal government affects local and state wildlife programs. As the saying goes,"Times are a changing".

I think it is important that those involved with some programs should realize that this is a fact in the way things are done in this day and age. You cannot be part of something to promote your state programs when after the fact the federal government can step in and say how you can do it.

It is interesting to have observed how the tentacles of the federal agencies have gotten bigger and bigger through the years while most states are struggling just to keep their DNR and other agencies staffed. This boils right down to the fact I talked about up above where they are now so involved with fish and wildlife programs within the states.

You want to remember that you as a tax payer are paying the bills for both the state and federal agencies, only you have way less control or say in what regulations the federal government places on things.

So when you complain and kick about what the DNR may be doing remember one of the worst things that could happen would be for Washington to get more and more control over everyday things that affect those of us that love the great outdoors.

This is the only kind of evolution we can document taking place right before our eyes.

STATE OF MICHIGAN
ALLISON GREEN, STATE TREASURER
LANSING

MO.	DAY	YR.	SOCIAL SECURITY	NAME	MAIL	GROSS	WARRANT NO.
11	01	73		WALKER JOHN A		531.63	DF05937

NET PAY	RATE OF PAY	REGULAR TIME	PREM. HRS.	SHIFT DIFF.	SHIFT DIFF. O.T.	RETIREMENT	F.I.C.A.	LTD. INS.
343.16	5.96	89.2 HRS				26.58		.24

HOSP. INS.	LIFE INS.	OTHER INS.	MAINT.	MISC.	FED. EXEMPTIONS	FED. INCOME TX	ST. EX.	ST. INCOME TX	CITY EX.	CITY INC. TX
1.45		1.70			84.50	M 05	59.61	5		11.73

Y.T.D. EARNINGS	Y.T.D. RETIREMENT	Y.T.D. F.I.C.A.	Y.T.D. FED. INCOME TX	Y.T.D. STATE TX	Y.T.D. CITY TX
2.66					
11,508.93	491.45	631.80	1,660.93	358.85	

PAY PERIOD	CITY TAX PAID TO
10/07-10/20	

STATE OF MICHIGAN
ALLISON GREEN, STATE TREASURER
LANSING

No. F393346

MO.	DAY	YR.	SOCIAL SECURITY	NAME	MAIL	RATE
6	08	67		WALKER JOHN A	414	2.55

GROSS	OVERTIME	LOST TIME	FT INCOME TX.	RET-SS	MISC.
204.00			20.95	15.10	35.60

CITY INCOME TX	HRA CSC	HRA OTHER	MAINT.	LIFE INS.	
8.25				.89	

CREDIT UNION	HOSP INS	NET PAY	YTD FED. INCOME TX	YTD EARNINGS
		123.21	250.56	2,442.40

PERIOD 05/14 TO 05/27   FED EXEMPT M 02
HAPPINESS IS...,YOUR SUGGESTION AWARD CHECK.

You notice the $2.55 an hour I was paid and I thought I was on top of the world with the best job anyone could have.

Chapter 6

Conservation Officer's Stories
Upper Michigan Tales from a Game Warden's Perspective

The Old Timers

The Conservation Officers that work the field today for the Michigan DNR have those that broke the trail to thank for the reputation they enjoy. The old game wardens were from a whole different time and had a totally different outlook on life.

Here are a few articles from a long time ago to better explain what it meant to be a Michigan game warden and the type families that were the officer's families.

Evolution of a Game Warden

Shintangle- sweet fern and bracken- smells good to a man who is accustomed to the stink of a fishing sloop. Solid ground feels good beneath one's feet after months of balancing one's self on the narrow deck of a rolling, pitching vessel.

And to Mark Crow the land looked good. The year was 1900. Mark-then 34- had been around. He'd seen a lot of the country traveling ahead of a circus, carrying a bill poster's brush and paste bucket. But he'd seen nothing that had looked as good to him as his home county of Grand Traverse. So he had returned, to sign on as a member of the crew of a trading and fishing vessel.

Had Big Territory

Mark had his share of courage. He was going to need it because he had decided he wanted to be a game warden. Lumbering operations still were being carried on. The country was full of hard, weather-beaten, red-blooded men. Fish and game were looked upon as every man's booty and game wardens were classed with the odoriferous animals that raided the settler's scantily populated chicken coops.

Mark's ambition was realized. State Game and Fish Warden Grant M. Morse appointed him as game warden for the northern third of the Lower Peninsula in October 1900.

This fact ought to qualify Mark as a veteran of the Conservation Department's law enforcement body- as, in fact, he is. He's nearly 74 now- one of the two oldest men in the service and is still actively carrying on the duties of a conservation officer in Grand Traverse County.

Was Law Enforcement Job

Seasoned in rough ways, Mark was given his credentials, a copy of the then meager fish and game laws, and he started to look around for his first victims. A game warden's job then, was strictly a law enforcement job. He had a big territory to cover and travel was slow. You used either a train, logging spur, horse, buggy or cutter, and in winter on snowshoes or a foot.

Mark got along fairly well in his area, learned something about the business of law enforcement and the temperament of the citizens of that day. Then, late in the first winter and along toward the spring breakup, he got a tip that certain men were fishing illegally on Big Mud Lake down around Interlochen.

If Mark disregarded that tip he wouldn't have to favor one foot today.

Unpleasant Duty

There was only one way to get to Big Mud Lake from Traverse City in those days and that was by horse and cutter and by foot over the hills and rough country roads. The few warm days had weakened the ice on the lakes and softened the crusted roads. It was 17 mile by cutter and two miles on foot but, undaunted, Mark started out. He reached the lake and found two men fishing through the ice illegally. Mark arrested them. He explains that in those days you had to take your men with you or else you never got them again so he walked them over to his cutter and loaded them in with himself sitting on their laps and handling the reins. In getting to his men and off the lake again he had broken through the ice and his legs and feet were a trifle wet. About this time the weather changed, the temperature began to go down and steel-tempered particles of snow began to strike the men's faces. Mark said the single horse blanket that covered them was inadequate for the job and his legs from the knees to feet stuck out. The 17-mile trip didn't look so good but he figured he had to get men to jail somehow. So they started out. Somewhere along the way he went in and borrowed a pair of woolen socks for one of the men who complained of cold feet. When they finally arrived and sought the warmth of the old jail; in Traverse City, Mark discovered that both his feet were frozen as was the flesh over his knees. He had been afraid to put up overnight at some settler's home because he didn't want to let the men out of his sight long enough to catch a few winks of sleep.

Mark Saves His Feet

Mark had a lot of trouble with those feet and finally wound up in Ann Arbor where he came out of a daze to discover he was being wheeled into an operating room where amputation was to be preformed. He roused, then, and refused to permit the operation. The doctors did something or other after that but eventually his toes got so stiff that he had to have one big toe removed so he could walk better. But today, although his toes are stiff, he carries himself like a man of 47 rather than one who is 74.

Incidentally, Mark says the two men he arrested were employed by a lumber company to supply its camp with fish. At the time, the lumber company had posted a $25 reward for the arrest and conviction of anyone fishing illegally.

After this experience Mark decided that, all in all, a game warden's life was no bed of roses. He stayed with the job however, for another two and a half years, at three dollars per day and expenses. But by 1903 he had made up his mind that the grass looked greener on the other side of the fence so he quit the service and started up a pony express business in Traverse City. This went fairly well for a few years and until horseless carriages began to fill the horizon and forced him to the conclusion that ponies were being force out.

At this time the old lure of the woods and the streams and the fascination of matching wits with those who break the law had been working on him. So in 1916 he again sought employment with the state.

On Job Again in 1917

In April, 1917, Mark once more proudly displayed a warden's commission and he was relieved to find that his assignment covered only Benzie, Leelanau, and Grand Traverse counties instead of a third of the southern peninsula. Many changes had taken place. Forest fires had swept over many abandoned acres after the departure of the lumberman. Settlers had occupied the better areas. More attention was being paid to natural resources, although the words were hardly understood as yet, and a much larger force of men was considered necessary to supply adequate protection for wildlife. The Public Domain Commission had been created and the thought of influential men had to converge into channels that were to lead in a few years to the creation of the present Department of Conservation.

Mark held the warden's commission until March 1, 1920. Model T's had appeared and traveling was simpler, more people were arriving to hunt and fish, more laws were being enacted, but, generally, the work was just as arduous.

Takes Charge of District

By 1920, the forest fire problem had become so important that districts had been organized for better protection and, as of March 1, Mark took over new duties as a district fire warden. In 1921, the present Conservation Department was formed and in 1922 Mark was appointed district warden in charge of game and fish and fire activities.

In 1923 legislation was enacted which definitely pegged the duties and responsibilities of citizens as concern forest fires, thus lifting a considerable part of the burden from the shoulders of men like Mark who were in charge of the various district into which previously forested areas were divided. It was about this time that Mark took charge of what is know now as District 12, the five counties of Leelanau, Grand Traverse, Wexford, Benzie, and Manistee.

By July 15, 1931, Mark was approaching 65 years of age. His burden of duties had become heavier. A district headquarters building had been erected and it was no longer necessary to use the best front room of his home as an office or to impress his wife into service as office assistant. A man had been placed in charge of fire as an assistant supervisor or warden. Commercial fishing was demanding a lot of law enforcements attention.

The department had gotten out of politics. (remember this line as you think of the DNR today) New faces appeared in supervisory roles. New ideas, more paper work, added responsibilities were the order of the day. New policies were born.

They Fought a Good Fight

And so Mark stepped down- turned over his command to a younger man and became a warden again, assigned to duties in Grand Traverse County under supervision of District 12 headquarters.

Only now he wasn't know as a game warden- he was a Conservation Officer. About this time several of his contemporaries relinquished supervisory burdens also to resume again the simpler duties of officers assigned to counties.

Mark and these others, had fought a good fight. He, and some of the others, are still in harness. He, and they, had laid the ground work, had felt out public sentiment, had toiled long hours, had performed arduous, dangerous tasks, had pioneered in stirring public consciousness and in enlisting public support of Conservation measures.

Theirs are the traditions. Theirs is the example which inspires the rookie conservation officer today.

(Taken from a August 1940 Conservation Magazine-by Harry L. Aldrich)

Some Remarks By an Old Game Warden

Here are some remarks attributed to Mark in articles I came across. I think they tell you what 100 years has done to the great outdoors

"I have seen the pigeons, the pine, the grayling and the sturgeon so common only the Indians would use them. We can't hope to get these back the way they were but what is left is still well worth saving. Michigan has many things of beauty and value and it is our responsibility to see that they are protected and developed.

We have made wonderful progress in recent years but there is still much to do."

Some Things Never Change only the Dates Do

"Back in 1900 or 1901 I had raided a hunter's camp and got out to the county seat with two hounds they had used to run deer, two rifles and a doe deer. I locked the dogs in a box stall in the livery barn, put the hunter's guns and my gun in the hotel office in care of the landlord, and billed the deer with the Adams Express Company."

"I got out the warrants, hired a team and driver and started back in the night in a sleigh to bring in the hunters. The driver had his "instructions" and drove me around all night without finding the hunter's camp, and we got back to the county seat in the morning with me almost froze. In the meantime, and while we were gone, friends of the hunters broke into the box stall and turned the dogs loose, got the guns from the hotel, someone had put mine under the safe and bent the barrel, and broke into the express office and stole the deer."

"The prosecuting attorney was a stock holder in the lumber company where the hunters were selling their deer. This was one case that never came to trial."

Marks adds, he had been tipped off to some wholesale spearing on Lake Leelenau and had been advised the law was not welcome in that area. Mark hitched up his buggy and made his way to a summer hotel on the shore of the lake, packing a 40-pound canvas canoe. The first night out, Mark says he saw so many lights on the water it looked like the fireflies had grown up and taken over the lake. He approached one boat with jack light blazing and with four occupants,"

One of the four jack lighters thought he heard a noise and mentioned the fact to his companions. Mark was sitting quietly in his canoe just outside the flare of light. The man in the rear of the boat picked up a rifle, later identified as a 38/56 and laid it across his knees, stating in a loud voice that if the blankety-blank warden came upon them he'd never live to tell about it.

Mark heard as he sat there in the dark and believed him, so he merely hung back in the shadows until the boat was drawn up to shore. He then landed down shore and walked towards the men. The rifle lay across the boat while they unloaded their duffle. Mark stepped out beside and seized the gun before they could reach it. Two of the men ran into the brush but he loaded the other two into their boat and escorted them to the hotel and eventually to court where they were released after payment of $220 fines. Mark says the men had 154 pounds of bass, full of spawn, a grain sack full of panfish, and one mammoth pike. Mark says the arrest stopped the spearing on the lake for some time.

Veteran Game Warden Wears Uniform on Visit to President.

On the LEFT SLEEVE of Conservation Officer Mark Craw's uniform are seven gold stars, representing 35 years of service besides the few he has accumulated towards another 5-year emblem. Half a lifetime in the service of the state has made the Traverse City officer proud of that uniform. To him it seemed only proper that he should appear in it at the White House when President Roosevelt presented to him, his daughter-in-law, and grandson, the Congressional Medal of Honor awarded posthumously to his son Colonel Demas T. "Nick" craw.

Stories of the accomplishments of Mark Craw's son are well know in Mark's home district, but the record is one of which all the state may be proud.

Colonel Craw was the first American to die in the battle for the liberation of French North Africa. Craw airfield at Port Lyautey, French Morocco, is named in his honor, and the No. 1 American grave there, decorated by the President on his Casablanca visit, is Colonel Craw's.

Mark believes that if his son had reached French army headquarters on the mission on which he met his death, fighting would have stopped the day it started, rather than three days later. The Colonel's party of three went ashore in the first wave, under shells fire from both ship and shore batteries, and in a car, smaller than a jeep and bearing French and American flags and the white flag of an emissary, they got many miles inland before a burst from a hidden machine gun killed Craw.

Colonel Craw knew he was taking a big risk, but he wanted to. He abandoned his neutrality long before his country did, and as an observer in the Mediterranean he was 136 times under fire flying wit the British. He was known in every RAF headquarters in the Middle East. At the time of the Albanian campaign, when he was U.S. attaché at Athens, he was decorated by the King of Greece.

His trail to the Middle East was by way of Singapore, China, Burma, India, Alexandria, and Cairo, and after the occupation of Greece he came back to Washington by the way of Turkey, Russia and Persia. He declined a safe job in this country to take the Morocco Assignment.

The Congressional Medal of Honor- the fifth awarded in this war-capped a military career that began with enlistment in the cavalry in Texas, training at West Point when General Douglas MacArthur was superintendent.

(Needless to say Colonel Craw was a son any father would be proud of and dad only thought it was fitting to wear the uniform he was so proud of to meet the President of out Nation.)

Way Before 9/11

The one thing I hear over and over falls into two types, there are those that tell me that they have been sitting in the same spot for a number of years and never see any deer and there are those that have had someone move right in on top of their hunting spot. These too are still sitting in the same spot even though there is someone sitting right next to them, so close that neither has had any luck in years.

My suggestion is really simple. Move!

I cannot believe those that have not had any luck in a place for years and still go back and sit there year after year.

It is kind of like the story I was told a while back about someone that had their "private" hunting spot spoiled. This will date some of us a little.

For those of us that are old fossils we remember when the way into hunting areas was by using the old railroad grades. But even before this there were those that actually used the railroads to get to and from an area. Some hunters even had their own "put-put" cars to travel on the tracks with.

But then times changed and the Sun Shine, Blaney, Haywire, Main Line and so many other tracks were pulled up and the old grades became 2-tracks back into the areas. In fact in some cases the then Conservation Department put in culverts and fixed up the grades to make areas more accessible for hunters. This did not go over too well with those hunters that had claimed some of these areas as their private hunting grounds. It did not matter if these areas were state or federal land.

It seems that there was this party over in the eastern part of Schoolcraft County that was really upset with the fact that he had lost his "private" hunting grounds. After brooding about it for a while he came up with a way of once again turning his "private" spot into an inaccessible area. So he went out and purchased a bag of dynamite and set out to blow up all the culverts the Conservation Department had placed on the grade.

It seems that everything went as planned and all the culverts were blown up and as he stood looking over his project at the last blown culvert he wadded up the bag that the dynamite had come in and threw it away.

Mission accomplished! There was only one problem. It seems when you went out to purchase dynamite you had to sign a receipt for it. Guess what was in the bag he had wadded up and thrown in the ditch?

Typical hunter when I was growing up.

Dedicated To

Book number nine in the *Tales from a game warden* series is dedicated to these three individuals that represent the many people and organizations that have helped me out with my books and the scholarship project. Without the help of people such as these I would have never been able to succeed. The more than $60,000 raised for the scholarship fund would not be anywhere near there without the help of those who have access to so many people through the media.

Mary Drier:

I started out my career with the then Michigan Department of Conservation stationed in the town of Caro located on the "Thumb" of Michigan's lower peninsula 30 miles east of Saginaw. When I was working there Caro was a little farm community where everybody seemed to know everyone. I always tell a person that was before they got a Wal-Mart and became a city.

When I was stationed there the local newspaper was owned by Rudy, who was a friend of law enforcement and every once in a while helped out at busy times as a part time dispatcher at the sheriff's department. After I left Caro for the U.P. the paper changed hands.

When I retired and started to self-publish my books I took a shot in the dark and sent a news release and some information to the Tuscola County paper in hopes they would be willing to help me out in letting those that lived in the "Thumb" area know about my books. Little did I know how important this would be.

First off Mary wrote an article for the Tuscola County Adviser that produced a good number of book sales for me. Later her article appeared in a number of other papers that covered the Thumb area of Michigan and this was something I never expected, but it sure covered a large area of Eastern Michigan for me.

Then the strangest thing happened, I started getting book orders from Indiana, Illinois, and other parts of Michigan from areas where I had never received orders from before. I finally asked one of those that called from Fort Wayne, Indiana how they had heard about my books. They told me that had read an article in the Farmer Advance Newspaper they received.

It seems that Mary had in the past sent articles to this newspaper when she felt it covered an area their readers would like. Once again it opened a whole new area for my books.

You know life can sure take some funny twists. A few years later I got to thinking of all that Mary had done for me and the scholarship project so I wanted to send her a thank you note. I wanted to make sure she was still where I could get hold of her so I typed her name in on the internet as a newspaper writer and the following article came up. I could not believe it because I was in high spirits when looking for information on Mary then it felt like I had been kicked in the stomach.

I have always wondered why it seems that some people that go out of their way to help others only to have such heavy loads to carry themselves.

Army Sgt. Charles A. Drier

Charles A. Drier was coming home in July for a joyous occasion: He would walk his mother down the aisle for her second marriage.

"He wasn't just my son," said his mother, Mary. "He was my best friend. I'll miss his smile, his compassion."

Drier, 28, of Tuscola, Mich., was killed May 24 when an explosive detonated near his vehicle in Bagdad. He was based at Fort Stewart.

Drier played football in high school and was known as a generous natural leader.

"He liked structure, discipline, tradition," said his former coach, Tim Travis.

The 1995 high school graduate enlisted in the Army in 2001 after stints as a cook and roofer. He saw the Army as a chance for college and a new career.

"He felt like his life was going nowhere," Mary Drier said. "There's nothing but dead-end jobs around here. He wanted his life to have a purpose, to have some meaning."

He aspired to be a writer.

"He was an avid reader and talked about writing a book," his mother said. "Fiction. He sent me some pages, and I was very impressed. I was looking forward to reading more, but..."

As I said I never had the oppertunity to meet Mary Drier for it seemed when I would stop by she was not in. This past winter (2007) I was asked to speak at an outdoor banquet down in the Thumb area town of Marlette. On the way back home I checked out my old stomping grounds and stopped by the Adviser hoping Mary would be in. She was and we had a good talk and I got to thank her face to face for all the help she had been.

But the best part was finding out that she has not changed. She is still going out of her way to help someone else. It seems that another mother, from Vassar a town about 30 miles away, had lost her son over in the war and called Mary to see if she could come down and visit her.

Mary told me she didn't know if she could, but being a mother who had been through it, and knowing another mother needed her she went down for a visit. She said we hugged and cried and had a sweet time together.

I think this tells you just the type person Mary is.

As I was working on this chapter I came across this on the internet and decided to put it in here so you could read it and see the type people I had the privilage of running into on my job. Some of the best people in our country enjoy hunting and fishing and the great outdoors.

Another Tuscola County boy.

VASSAR -- The Esckelson family is mourning the death of Marine Cpl. Christopher E. Esckelson in Iraq -- yet thankful the injuries to his second cousin, Army Reserve Staff Sgt. Ricky "Rick" E. Esckelson, aren't life-threatening.

"Chris always wanted to be a Marine," said his father, David E. Esckelson, 48, of Vassar.

Chris Esckelson lived for the Marine Corps motto of Semper Fidelis (Always Faithful. He had his own creed: Semper Auxiliarius (Always Helping), his father said.

"He eventually wanted to be a doctor and was saving money to become one," he said.

Meanwhile, Ricky Esckelson is mending while awaiting word whether he will recuperate in Germany or try to heal where he in Iraq, his family said.

Chris Esckelson died while helping fellow Marines -- killed by a direct hit to his torso from enemy fire in an intense firefight, his father said, relaying to The Saginaw News what military personnel told him.

"From what I was told, six went down," he said. "My son was a squad leader and was trying to help his men -- he was trying to get a fellow Marine to safety when he was hit. He was pronounced dead within three minutes of getting hit."

Serving with the 1st Battalion of the 24th Marines in Iraq, he died around 2:45 p.m. Wednesday, three days shy of his 23rd birthday.

David Esckelson was fishing Thursday on the banks of the Saginaw River with friends when he got a cell phone message that Marines were at his home looking for him.

"My heart just dropped," he said. "As a dad with a son in the Marines, that's what you always fear -- that the military will come.

"Well, they definitely came. There were five of them. They're quite a group."

David Esckelson's former wife -- Chris Esckelson's mother -- Michelle "Mitzi" M. Hill, 48, of Vassar, works as a letter carrier for the U.S. Postal Service and was on her mail route when she got a call from her co-workers.

"The military showed up at my house, where my mother is staying with us," Hill said.

"My mother told (the Marines) where I work, and they went there. The clerks there called me and asked where I was, saying they need to bring me something.

"I just knew it was bad news -- my mom or my son -- because there was nothing they had to bring me. So they came and got me."

Hill, in turn, broke the news to her son's girlfriend of three years, Samantha Reasner, 19, of Owosso.

"She was over (Thursday) night. She was a mess at first, but she's doing better now."

Hill said she didn't want her son to enlist.

"He wanted to earn money for college," she said. "We were worrying about what might happen.

"But he said, 'Nope, I want to be a Marine.' That was what he wanted.

"He was a very smart kid, I feel he could have gotten scholarships if he applied himself. But he said even if he graduated

45

valedictorian, he still would have joined the Marines."

Chris Esckelson loved sports, she said. In high school, he was outfielder and catcher for the baseball team for four years, was defensive tackle on the football team for four years and played basketball for two years.

He was also an avid hunter, bagging deer and turkey and planned to go bear hunting with his father and brother, Craig E. Esckelson, 19.

The brothers have a sister, Kerry M. Esckelson, 17, a junior at Vassar High School. The family attends St. Michael's Lutheran Church in Richville.

Chris Esckelson graduated from high school in spring 2002 and in October joined the Marines, Hill said. In between, he took classes at Delta College.

He shipped over to Iraq at the end of September and was supposed to return in April.

For his birthday, today, his mother e-mailed him that she was going to treat him to dinner and shopping.

"I was going to take him to Zehnder's restaurant, where he worked as a waiter, and then to Abercrombie & Fitch (at Fashion Square Mall) to go clothes shopping, since he worked there, too," she said. "He always liked to look sharp.

"He was a go-getter, a leader. He was outgoing, was well-liked, had lots of friends and loved by lots of family," she said. "He believed in what he was doing. His proudest thing was to be a Marine."

Now, the family is making funeral arrangements.

Members plan to contact Martin Funeral Home in Vassar for services, with burial at Riverside Cemetery in Vassar.

"That's the trouble with the military," David Esckelson said. "They can send (my son) to the front lines in a day-and-a-half, but it takes seven to 10 days to bring him home.

"That's going to be a long seven to 10 days.

"He was a hero," his father said. "He was definitely a hero.

"He was more than a son; he was my best friend."

Buck LeVasseur:

Buck is just a little guy and when the snow gets deep up along Lake Superior you may take a chance of losing him out in the woods. But buck is probably one of the best known men in the whole U.P. It has been a U.P. tradition on Monday evenings to sit down in front of the TV and get set for Buck and his Discovering show. It has been this way for more years than I can recall.

When my first book (*A Deer Gets Revenge*) came out I had no idea how you went about peddling a book. I just placed a number of boxes in the trunk of my car and started out to see what happened. I had talked to a couple of local businessmen one of which told me, "John, the best advice I can give you is to just sell them one at a time." So off I went.

I knew about and watched Discovering on TV 6 for years so I just thought the natural thing to do was stop off up in Marquette and give a copy to Buck. I had been told by a number of the "Exspurts" that it was almost impossible to have anything done on a book on Buck's Discovering show. But what did I really have to lose.

Just a short time later I received a call from Buck and we met so he could do a piece on his program about my book. I happened to be up in the Copper County at Houghton where I watched it in a motel room. It was an excellent piece that hit on my growing up in Ontonagon, later working as a Michigan conservation officer, and how the stories for the book had come about.

I really had no idea how big of an impact being on Buck's show would have, but as I traveled around asking businesses if they would be willing to sell my book, I heard over and over, "We saw you on Discovering."

In fact, there were a number of times right after the show was aired where I was standing in a bookstore or a business that sold books waiting to talk to the manager when someone would come in and ask the manager, "Do you have that book by a game warden that was on Buck's Discovering show on TV 6?"

More often than not, the owner would have a look on his face like "a what book"! I could then say, "Maybe I can help you out." I would show them a copy of my bright, hunters orange book. It sure improved my chances of getting them to try and sell a few books for me.

Through the years Buck has done a number of features about my books on his show and has had a real impact on their success. For this, all the students that have been helped by the scholarship fund along with this humble book writer, we would like to say, "Thank you Buck for all your help."

Dave Richey:

In this world you see so many people that get to the top of the mountain in their profession and forget those that are still struggling or trying to get started in theirs. Then once in a while you come across someone who is at the top of the heap and remembers those that helped him get there and is more than happy to pass on their help to others.

Dave Richey was just such a person. In our state the big newspaper is the Detroit Free Press and for years Dave was the main outdoor writer for them. For years I had read his articles each week to get his perspective on the outdoors and what we could look forward to when the hunting or fishing seasons were right around the corner.

You would think that someone like Dave would be kind of highfalutin after all the success he had and those he was rubbing shoulders with. In so many places this is what you see happen. But not here, he is still just a hunter and fisherman that loves the great outdoors.

Maybe it was because with Dave there had always been a team. You see he had a twin brother who was also a successful outdoor writer and for years and years they were both leaders in the Michigan's outdoor media. Working as a conservation officer I was always well aware of the Richey brothers even though we had never crossed paths as long as I was working.

So once again when my first book came out I took a shot in the dark and sent a copy along with a news release to Dave Rickey at the Detroit Free Press. In was only a dream in ever hoping to get my book mentioned in the biggest paper in the state. Little did I realize that during the fall when Dave published a list of recommended books as Christmas gifts he made mention of my book *A Deer Gets Revenge*. Needless to say this article went all over the state and led to a good number of sales.

(Let me just say here that Dave Otto from the Green Bay Press Gazette did the same thing on his recommended Christmas reading list. Also Richard Smith the outdoor writer from Marquette made mention of my book in his article in the MUCC Magazine. All in all these three articles led to the sale of hundreds and hundreds of books through the years. The outdoor writing fraternity is a special group of people.)

Maybe Dave himself better explains what I am trying to say in an article he wrote. This article was for the Outdoor Unlimited Magazine, the publication for Outdoor Writers Association of America March 2007 issue.

In it he wrote: "It's been said that what goes around, comes around. I'm living proof of how that principle works. The more one gives to others and to the organization, the more that comes back to the giver."

"I'm always happy to help others, and, in turn, others have helped me." (Is this not a lost art in so many areas of out life today?)

"I actually endorse the principle of giving more than I take."

'I also love to mentor people during the year and at present am helping four people, three from Michigan and one from Wisconsin."

I think these quotes help to tell the heart and soul of a true outdoor writer. It also better explains just why such a man would help an unknown, self-published, author from the backwoods of Michigan's Upper Peninsula who just had a dream.

49

I just wanted to use these three people to help you better understand just why things have gone the way they have for me and my books. I could sit here and list a number of people that were willing to help, but it is impossible to list them all, so with these three I say "Thank you" to all of you out there.

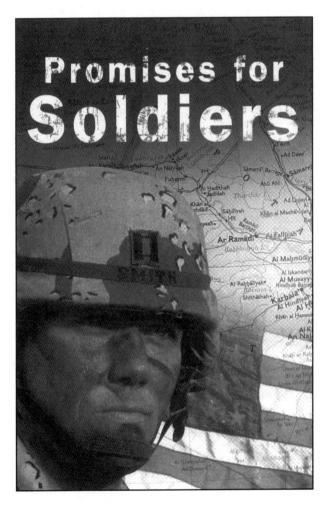

We should all be thankful for those that help us.

Conservation Officer's Stories **Upper Michigan Tales from a Game Warden's Perspective**

Some Things Are Just Meant To Be

No matter how hard game wardens try at times things do not seem to work out right. But then again at times it seems they just receive gifts from heaven.

Where Were You Again?

Back to the serious stuff in the case of the blown tread.

It seems that this rather notorious party that likes to supplement his feeding habit with wild game and fish was up to his old tricks. This night he was working at his trade rather hard and had a good thing going when all of a sudden he realized that he was not the only party in the area and this was not good.

But this guy always had an escape plan set up just in case things were to go wrong and on this evening he put the plan into high gear. Off he went through the woods running as fast as he could, and he had a lot of experience at this. With the game warden in hot pursuit he cut across a swamp and came up behind a farm and went up in the barn and hid in the hay loft. It looked like this night the guys wearing the black hats were going to win because the local wardens had no idea where he was. He knew every trail through the woods and often he had thought of using this barn for just such an occasion as this.

So he curled up and spent the night sleeping in the hay loft. It was better doing this even if it was cold and not the most comfortable night he had ever spent than getting down and maybe getting caught.

As morning rolled around he heard the milk truck coming up the lane to get the milk from the farm where the barn was. He climbed down and hooked a ride back to town on the milk truck bragging about how he had beat the game warden at their game this time.

In fact, he told this half of the story to anybody that would listen, and quit there, but if the game warden was around he had to tell the rest of the story.

It seems that when he was cutting through the swamp heading for the trail he lost his brand new shoe in some black muck! In fact he could not find it, and the game wardens could be seen coming through the woods with their flashlights so he took off without it and got away.

There was one slight problem! It seems that the game wardens following along behind him failed to catch him, but they did find his shoe stuck in the mud. After giving up trying to find our poacher the officers took his shoe and headed home.

The next morning one of the wardens was looking at the shoe and realized that it was made by a company that specialized in shoes mostly sold by mail order. So he looked the shoe over real good and came across a serial number on the inside of the shoe. He made contact with the company and they sent him a copy of the sales receipt for the person that had ordered the pair of shoes.

Guess who was really surprised when the local warden knocked on his door holding his lost shoe and the sales slip.

Tell Me You Didn't

It seems that there was this hunter that had an over abundant amount of luck while out deer hunting. In fact his luck had been so good he had more bucks lying in front of him than he had kill tags to place on them.

So being the ingenious guy he was he figured out how to solve the problem. He got on his cell phone and called his wife at home. He told her that she needed to find someone who had an extra kill tag for a deer that he could use because he had an extra deer without a tag.

He told the wife where he was and how they could find him once she got hold of them. It was just about an hour and a half later when he heard a vehicle come down the road and stop then a door slam. He got up and walked out to the road to meet the help that was on the way. Just as he broke into the open onto the road he came face to face with the local game warden. Needless to say this was the last person in the world he wanted to see.

It not only seemed that the game warden knew right where he was but was not there by chance seeing he knew all the facts as to just why our overly successful hunter was there.

It seemed that right after he had talked to his wife and told her he needed her to find someone with an extra deer tag she figured out the best way to handle her husband's problem.

She figured if there was anyone that could help him out with getting him an extra deer tag it had to be the local DNR officer so she called him. It seems that he was more than happy to head out to where her husband was so she filled him in with the directions he had given her.

For some reason I kind of figured that this was not really what the husband had in mind when he called his wife for help.

Maybe There's a Better Way

Did you hear the story about the hunter that went to sit in his blind on opening day of hunting season and found someone sitting in it trying it out?

Well, it seems that this individual went into his blind which he has had in the same place for years to sit on the opening morning of the firearm deer season. As he walked up he sees this party sitting in his blind. He mentioned to the guy that it was his blind and he had been hunting this spot for years. In fact that was his bait pile out there in front of his blind. In fact, he stated if you look right there it even has my name written on it.

The party looked at him and asked, "This is state land here isn't it?" "So this means first come, first serve and I plan on spending the rest of the day here.

It was obvious that this hunter, even though he knew it was someone else's blind was not about to move.

So the owner of the blind simple stated, "You are right this is state land so I don't want to get in trouble leaving a deer blind set up here so I plan on removing it the best and quickest way I can."

53

He then left and went back to his pickup, where in the back he had his woods working gear. He reached into the back and got out his 5-gallon can of chain saw gas. He then headed back into his deer blind. When the hunter that was sitting in his blind looked out and saw him coming with a 5-gallon gas can, and knowing the mood he was in, he had the sudden inspiration to hunt on the other side of the creek and get there as fast as he could move.

A Detroit Hunter

I don't want to see everybody get down on life so I figure I had better tell you a good old game warden story.

It seems that there were a couple of game wardens having breakfast in a restaurant in a small town when a successful hunter fresh from the asphalt jungle of Detroit came in for breakfast. The only way you would ever guess this party was a hunter was the fact he had stopped at the local sporting good store on the way north and purchased a red and black plaid hunting outfit that made people realize you were an official deer hunter.

This party came in and sat down and soon was informing anyone who would listen about the trophy buck he had out in the back of his pickup. The more he talked the better and better the story got and in fact he was starting to get on the nerves of the other hunters in the restaurant.

The two game wardens got done with their breakfast and went out to the parking lot and looked at the buck in the back of the pickup that was parked to the side of the restaurant. They figured they may as well have a little fun with this Detroit hunter so they took the buck out of the back of his pickup and replaced it with a doe out of the trunk of their car.

They then returned to the restaurant and confronted this Detroit hunter about the fact that the deer in the back of his pickup was not a buck but a doe! And seeing it was a doe they would have to check his anterless deer permit. The man insisted it was not a doe but a nice trophy buck. They again told him they had just looked at the deer and it was indeed a doe, not an antlered buck at all and they needed to see a permit for it.

Finally they convinced this Detroit hunter to come out and look at the deer with them. Out he came with all the others that were in the restaurant to see this trophy buck that was now said to be an anterless deer.

They walked around the restaurant and the party stepped up on the back bumper of his pickup to look at the deer. He then reached in and lifted it's head and before the game wardens could say anything he blurted out, "Those guys sold me a doe after I paid them $50 for a trophy buck!" Woops!

Needless to say he had never even looked at the deer that was loaded into his pickup after purchasing it from one of the locals.

King Smelt Comes Again

Up from the winter chilled waters of the Great lakes stream the silvery hordes of the smelt. And ready on the bank with dip nets of all sizes and shapes are hundreds of Michigan fishermen, addicts of this newest form of Michigan fishing.

Chapter 9
Conservation Officer's Stories **Upper Michigan Tales from a Game Warden's Perspective**
A Dangerous Job

Working as a game warden can be one of the more dangerous jobs there is. You are out there in all kinds of weather in all kinds of conditions. You are also using almost every kind of equipment there is and in some cases, especially in years past, not the best for what you are trying to undertake.

How They Died

I was reading an article about Conservation Officers that have lost their lives in the line of duty and by far the main cause of death for these officers was drowning. According to what I read a total of 170 officers lost their lives due to drowning. This is almost 90% of all the officers that lost their lives.

If you read about the officers that lost their lives due to drowning you soon find out that a good number of them were trying to or had rescued someone and then lost their life.

There was an officer in California who was in an area where there were two young boys and their mother who were caught in an ocean rip tide. They had tried to rescue them with the aid of a boat but it was too rough so the officer jumped in and managed to get the three to safety when a large wave tossed him into a jetty taking his life.

A Conservation Officer from Kentucky drowned while trying to rescue a young man that had fallen overboard.

There was a U.S. Fish & Wildlife Officer on board Flight 93 on 9/11 that crashed into the field in Pennsylvania. There is reason to believe, though nobody will ever know for certain, that this officer was one of those involved in rushing the cockpit to try and take the plane back. He was on his way home from a vacation.

These are things people generally never hear about. Like the Sergeant with the Indiana DNR who drowned while trying to save two of his fellow officers who had fallen in dangerous, swirling water during a training exercise.

Then there was a Fish Warden from Pennsylvania who with two other officers was in a boat on a rain-swollen river when it overturned. This officer had just about reached shore and safety when he heard his two partners calling for help and drowned when he decided to return and help them.

One man who had made the phone call that caused an officer his life after he rescued three people wrote: "We often hear comments directed at firemen, lifeguards, harbor patrol and other safety professionals about the ease of their jobs. In the absence of catastrophe, some people assume their work is rather inconsequential. But those of us who have been saved... know the real truth. And the truth is that if 364 days go by without a incident, and on the 365th, that man or woman has to break thru a burning door, or swim out through the swells on a rough day, they earn everything we pay them in that moment. For the officer's and his family, that debt, in fact, can never be paid, but we will always understand the value of his commitment."

It is one thing to give your life for a friend or family member who you know and love, but it is a totally different type person who is willing to jump into a swollen river or an ocean rip-tide to try and rescue someone they do not even know.

I have always said, and wrote about this fact in my books, that most of the old time Conservation Officers were like a family to each other. When you consider this I can picture the officers that gave up their lives trying to help a buddy in trouble. There was a type of camaraderie back in those days that seems to be lost in so many ways in this day and age.

I guess another true way of showing the character of so many Conservation Officers is to understand how many of them have or are serving over in Iraq and other war zones as members of the National Guard. I think this also shows the heart of these officers and their love for out nation and the things we get to enjoy.

Not Only Up Here

Well, up here in Yooperland is it any real surprise when spring arrives with 5-6 inches of that white stuff? The good thing is it wasn't big fluffy flakes or we would have had three feet of snow. If you are a true Yooper you can only hope that the snow we had last weekend was winters last gasp and spring weather is on the way now.

You that are still trying to catch a few fish you sure want to be careful in places with that heavy wet snow we got and the warming effect underneath. It is crazy but ice conditions can really change this time of year while all the time from the surface they look the same. It seems there are always some fishermen that either gets trapped out on an ice flow or they drive out and a big crack springs up between them and the shore.

I guess one thing that always bothered me was the fact when this happens because someone does not use their head there are others that literally have to risk their life trying to get them off the ice. As I said in the Fish Report a few weeks back a large percentage of game wardens that lose their life on the job lose it in drowning. A good number of these are while trying to help someone else out. Before you do something that could get you or someone else in trouble stop and ask yourself just how much a few fish are really worth.

In continuing with the dangers that always surround the job of a game warden working out in the field it has always been no secret that there are always those out there that have problems with the hunting and fishing laws. This can be either in the bag limits, the methods of harvesting, or even the seasons themselves. The one point that really amazes me is the fact that so many of the officers that lost their lives in the line of duty did so on a minor violation.

There was an officer in Pennsylvania that spotted two men spearing fish and found one did not have a fishing license. While he was talking to him the other man grabbed his gun and shot him. The officer died 28 days later.

There was also an officer in Kentucky shot three times in the chest after issuing a fishing violation. One of the darkest days in game warden history came in Minnesota where three officers conducting

59

a routine interview with some commercial fishermen were shot and killed.

I guess even here in Michigan if you go back and check the records most of the officers who lost their lives in the line of duty did so while trying to enforce a minor conservation law violation. One officer up here in the U.P. lost his life while checking someone with untagged traps. Then there were two officers that lost their lives while checking on someone trapping out of season.

If you stop and think about what the fines were back when a lot of these incidents took place the lives of the officer's end up being only worth a few dollars. And I mean very few dollars.

The one fact a person always wants to remember, from both sides, is the fact that an officer in some cases the way things fall into place does not know what to expect. This and the fact so many of the people they are checking are in possession of firearms whether they be hunting or fishing. Another fact is that in so many cases in today's world you have really no idea where drugs may be involved with those you are checking.

You can laugh, but I have been out there a number of times when fishermen, hunters, and even trappers figured while they were out in the great north woods what better time to smoke a little pot or drop a few pills to really enjoy things. When this is the case an officer never knows how they will react when this comes up.

This being the case, officers have to try and read those they are checking as to how they will react as he talks to them. This and the fact that there are so many people that hunt and fish that feel they cannot do it without a beer in their hand. Speaking from experience it does not make your day when you take a party from Illinois back to camp so they can post bond rather than go to jail and find a crew of 8-10 buddies that have been sitting around drinking all weekend. The party you are doing a favor for rather than taking him to jail knows you are giving him a break, but try explaining this to his drunken buddies! Needless to say I usually lucked out and there was at least one in the crew that understood that if they did not like the fact that their buddy was being given a chance to stay out of jail we could see that he didn't.

What makes a game wardens job all the harder is the fact that 90% of the violations he comes across amount to no more than a speeding ticket but for some reason people hate to gets caught messing up while enjoying the outdoors. This has not changed since the first game wardens were appointed by the counties to enforce the game and fish laws.

For The Better?

The job is not going to get any easier down the road with all the changes we are seeing in our nation.

I would like to mention something rather interesting. We have all heard about the problem with all the illegal aliens coming into our country. Would you believe this has affected DNR law enforcement so much that some states have had to send their officers to school to learn enough Spanish to be able to communicate with them because they do not speak English? I have to wonder how they managed to pass the hunter safety course or is this given in Spanish also? It sure makes for an interesting world we live in today and in some cases a rather scary one for the officers out there.

You have to remember that so many of these people have not grown up with our outdoor values. They grew up in a whole different world and this can affect how they hunt, fish, and react when checked by an officer.

I get asked all the time if I am sorry I retired and I always reply, "No, it was a great job, but there are just too many changes out there for an old fossil like me." I guess the fact that today's officers have to worry about speaking Spanish is another change I am sure I could not handle. It was time to get out.

Brings Back Some Memories

| *Conservation Officer's Stories*
Upper Michigan Tales from a Game Warden's
Perspective |

| **Some of My Favorite People-"Exspurts"** |

No matter how many years go by some things never seem to change. It seems that the only thing is that the goof-ups are a lot bigger and cost a lot more money. Here are a couple of items to prove my point.

| **Some Facts Then a Moose Attack** |

You know it is really funny how the twist and turns of life and nature always seem to work. There are those years when you have all kinds of success trapping but you wonder if you are going to receive enough for your furs to cover your gas cost. Then there are those years when the price of furs is going through the roof but you have to really work for each critter you catch. Such was the case this year.

I was reading an article where they were getting as much as $11 per muskrat. Where just a few years ago you were lucky to get $3. This year (2007) Michigan should ship over 500,000 pelts, 6,000 muskrat pelts were sold at the Clare auction. There is no shortage of raccoons around the state and this is good news for trappers. The average the trappers received for raccoon was $11 with a high of $24.

Michigan has produced some prime gray fox pelts and they were going for a high of $38 with an average of $30. A good number of these pelts are being shipped to China and some feel that this is the reason that the fur market was so high this year. You have to remember that one of the reasons the price of furs bottomed out a few years ago was the breakup of the Soviet Union. Like I said life can be interesting.

They are saying that the reason that fur numbers were way down on those that live in creeks or dams is because of the drought in some areas. It will be interesting to watch and see where things go in the next couple of years.

They still have a good market for red squirrels and there seems to be no shortage of these little critters in most areas.

I hear that the Natural Resource Commission may be having trouble with their math as was pointed out in the Fish Reports a while back. They are now talking about still allowing you to take two bucks, but one has to be during bow season and the other during firearm. I ask you does this not still make two bucks.

The bad thing about this whole deal is that it is a proven fact that fewer than 6% of all the hunters out there even bother to take the second buck. That's right just 6%! So as you can see this has become a political issue not a biological one. This is what makes the deer program too hard for those that are trying their best to manage it the right way.

I also found it interesting when I read on the internet the other day where Colorado is spending $160,000 on emergency feeding of wildlife with the stormy weather and all the snow they have received. What's wrong with this picture, don't they know it won't work and that there is no justified reason to help starving wildlife out during the winter. If you don't believe me just ask the "Exspurts" here in Michigan.

So you think you had a bad day. Did you hear about the moose that brought down a helicopter? It seems that an Alaska wildlife biologist shot a moose to tranquilize it. The moose figured that if this big bug was going to shoot darts at it he may as well go down fighting. So he charged the helicopter hitting it and damaging it so that it was forced to the ground. The moose was hurt so bad by the spinning rotors it had to be euthanized.

I find the most amazing part of the story. "As the animal got closer and closer to going down, an animal sort of loses its thinking-its ability to rationalize what's in its best interest," the regional supervisor stated.

Now I think this comment tells all of us one of the biggest problems we all have with the way things are looked at in today's world. I am going to try and put this supervisor's remark in Yooper terms so you can understand what this college educated person is really trying to say.

Mr. Moose thinks after just being shot by a dart. "Ouch, someone just stuck me! It looks like it came from that helicopter over there. Oooo I feel sleepy! I would like to charge that helicopter and fix their wagon, but if I did I just might get hurt and then they would have to put me to sleep for good. Man! I really feel sleepy now maybe I had better lay down. No! Those turkeys shot me with a dart so I may as well go for it!"

Now does any "normal" person really think a moose can stop and reason things out in life?

Don't Hit That Button!

As you read my books and the Fish Report you will soon realize that some of my favorite people are the "Exspurts" of this world. Someone sent me the following article on e-mail and it brought back memories. This is not the first time this has happened. In one state it seems that the "Exspurts" decided to bring all the years of data collected on bear and deer season up into the computer age.

It seems they hired some "Exspurts" to take all the old records and files and transfer them over to computer files. This was bound to make life a lot simpler and make all these records more accessible. It seems that everything was going along fine and all the records were now on the computer. With this done all the old boxes of cards and files were sent off to the dump.

But! Then it seems that for some reason all the records now on the computer disappeared and either were deleted or sent off into the distant world of computer outer space never to be found again. All the years of valuable data were lost forever.

As I read the following article I thought, "Do things really ever change?"

Wow! Computer "Exspurt" deletes $38 billion worth of records!

Alaska: Perhaps you have been there working on your computer and had that sick feeling when a single woops accidentally deleted hours and hours of work. Then if you think you had a bad day think of the guy that lost a $38 billion account from the hard drive.

This is what happened to a computer "Exspurt" reprogramming a disk drive at the Department of Revenue up in Juneau. While

65

doing what should have been routine maintenance on the program, our "Exspurt" mistakenly deleted all the applicant information for an oil-funded account. The cream of the crop the biggest perks in all of Alaska from an oil program was gone.

Was not this bad enough? Not really because our "Exspurt" managed to do the same things on the backup drive as well. A prime example of two wrongs do not make matters right.

There was still hope of being able to make things right with some back up tapes only to find out these were no good either.

"Nobody panicked, but we instantly went into planning for the worst-case scenario," said the director of this unit. This "Exspurts" mess cost the department more than $200,000 but they still hoped to recover $38 billion.

They called in the real Exspurts from some of the biggest computer companies only to find out their worst nightmares were about to come true.

Almost a years worth of work and almost a million electronic images that had been scanned into the program were somewhere out there in fiber space floating around. And now the only backup was hundreds of boxes of paper forms that they would have to once again scan into a computer.

We had to bring that paper back to scan and send it through again. Then we had to rework the program to tie everything back together again.

Exspurt: 1+1=1

Maybe this is one of the reasons that so many state agencies have become so top heavy in the last few years. The "Exspurts" trying to undo the problems created by other "Exspurts in the system.In talking to some hunters and listening to some speaking on the radio I have come to some interesting conclusions. The first, is there are a lot of hunters out there that never passed math. I have heard over and over from some of these hunters where when you add 1 and 1 you end up with 1.

They will tell you that they are against the two buck law! This is the cause of all the problems with life there are out there. **But!** Then in the next breath they will state, "I got a nice 6-point with my bow, and am hoping for a nice wall hanger with my firearm license." Now this is one of those cases where 1 plus 1 equals 1.

But they are against the hunter that does not bow hunt and takes two bucks with his firearm. This is a case where 1 plus 1 equals 2 and this is not right. Now I ask you did not both hunters remove 2 deer from the deer herd?

If you add to the factor that a lot of bow hunters take their buck during the main part of the rut you have to wonder if their whole goal is really, "They" should not be allowed to take 2 bucks because I want it left there for me to have a crack at. It sure makes one wonder.

Now before you get mad I both bow and firearm hunt, but I have always said that some of those "Exspurts" out there amaze me.

The other thing that has come to light are those hunters that believe in the "deer fairy". All during the winter we heard where there was not a deer left on the planet and now for the most part hunters are seeing a good number of deer and even a number of bucks. It must be that the good deer fairy felt bad after last deer season so made a lot more deer for this time around.

Really, if you read last years "Fish Reports" we talked about how the deer migration routes where they were tore up more than I had observed in a number of years. I even went as far as to say how many small tracks there were along some of these trails.

Who Was That Again?

I was reading some reports on the pollution in the great lakes and the warning about eating fish caught there. Now the first thing that really struck me was the fact that the headlines insinuated that if one was to eat fish caught in the great lakes they could die!

I wanted to find out what the report for Lake Michigan and Superior were seeing these two are the ones most of us are affected by. For the life of me I could not find a report that would state in laymen's terms what direction the pollution problems are going. One little blurp said that Lake Superior was better than it was during the last test. But how much better and in what areas? Lake Michigan, I could not find anything specific on it that explained what they were talking about.

Now even Eino and Teivo know that if one is going to put a headline on something that would get any fisherman's attention they could at least attach a copy of the information on the study to the article.

I did find out that two of the great lakes big problem is the pollution from Canada.

One thing in the article, and this is where we are going to get deep and theological, was the fact that wild birds and animals are causing more of the pollution than these "Exspurts" thought.

Now Eino has two questions for you.

First, are these not the same people that want every creature out there protected? If they had their way there would be no hunting season and all the fishing would be catch and release. Now what's wrong with this picture?

Second, do not these environmental "Exspurts" know who is really in charge of the wildlife population out there? In areas where there is so much wild land and so many weather factors around the Great Lakes that control population growth, who is in charge of nature? No, it's not Al Gore!

Chapter 11

Conservation Officer's Stories **Upper Michigan Tales from a Game Warden's** **Perspective**

A New Buddy

I guess if you grow up loving the great outdoors you also grow up needing to have a buddy to keep you company. You that have read some of my other books know I had a "Golden" named Rocky for a long time. When Rocky's end came I wasn't too sure if I wanted to get another dog. But in life sometimes things just happen.

I have always said that if it was a perfect world we lived in, a guys hunting dog would live as long as his master did. There is just something about a hunter and his dog that become a team no matter how the day goes or if they have any luck. It is just a matter of being able to get out into the field together.

Jupiter

Well, a lot of you years back read in my books about my dog Rocky. When Rocky got where he had to be put asleep I never really had any interest in getting another dog. In life it seems that there are some things that can never be replaced and to me Rocky was one of these.

But the other day in one of my weaker moments I saw a note on a bulletin board about someone that had a registered golden retriever to give away. I told myself I was not interested, but I made the mistake of telling Wifee about this dog.
I figured it would already be gone so forgot about it until Wifee talked to my daughter who was Rocky's companion. She, who now has a golden of her own, said, Dad you have to find out about this dog." I figured all right it will be gone and besides there are requirements that have to be met before I get another dog.

So Wifee called about the dog. The first problem was the dog was still available. The second item to be met was that he was full blooded and they had the papers on him. The third was that he

69

was already house broke and used to being indoors. I could see the writing on the wall about this time. But maybe the next requirement would make it so I would not take the plunge and get another dog.

I did not want to get another dog where they were at the age where after you got really used to them and they became your buddy they were at the age where you had to watch them getting old. But when I asked how old this dog was we were told 14 months. Then we made the biggest mistake of all and went to look at him.

A short, and I mean short, time later we returned home with a new addition. Now we have Jupiter as part of our household. Can you believe this?

So here I am once again the proud owner of a Golden Retriever for Wifee and I to enjoy. Now when I go out for my daily walk I have a buddy to keep me company. Could life get any better up here in God's Country? A man and his dog taking a walk through the woods and getting to enjoy all nature has given us.

A Dog's Beauty Shop

Of course after getting him out in the woods this week where you have an old fossil like me and a 15 month old dog it make one wonder. In fact I was wondering if maybe a small dose of Ritalin would slow him down just a little so I could at least stay in sight of him.

He really does not get far from you, it's just that he covers ground faster than my body can turn and keep up with him. But that's not the worst of it. I almost had to turn in my Yooper passport for something that happened a week back.

You have to remember that I grew up in the time period where a dog was just your dog. He had his own room, usually outside. If mom couldn't find us boys chances were we were in the dog house playing with the dogs. He had his choice of what he got to eat. Sometimes a lot, sometimes not so much it depended how hungry all the rest of us were because he got what was left over. Nobody even heard of buying dog food made just for dogs. It seems things were a tad bit different back then.

But that is not the only change. Would you believe when we went down to see my daughter she figured that Jupiter ought to go to a doggie beauty parlor! Now you have to be kidding me! What red blooded, all American Yooper would allow his dog to be taken to a have a bath-shampoo, checkup, and his hair and toe nails trimmed? Man, you could ruin a good hunting dog doing this. He would be too embarrassed to go out in the woods if word ever got out about him going to a doggie beauty shop.

But guess what? The vote on doing this was two to one and I was the one on the, "your vote doesn't count" end. So if you should see an embarrassed Golden Retriever around town you will know who he belongs to.

Our new buddy, Jupiter

These Conservation Officers have served for a total of 514 years: Front row (l-r) Lindgren-28, Craw-31, Wolters-22, Hicking-25, Strough-20, Barrow-20, McLean-16, Calkins-13 Center: (l-R) cronk-24, Heikkila-21, Buzzard-26, Frisbey-9, Aldrich-21, Andrews-35, Beach-21, MacDonald-19, Back: Dockham-18, Winey-21, Joslin-18, Kahl-18, Fuehr-18, White-26, Peabody-23, Benjamin-21

| *Conservation Officer's Stories*
Upper Michigan Tales from a Game Warden's
Perspective |
| **Some Ifens** |

| **With A Game Warden** |

Ifen, you understand the game wardens are not mind readers, but the closest thing there is to it.

Ifen, you understand that game wardens like sports too, so it is really bad to violate on Sundays or Monday nights when the Packers or Lions are playing.

Ifen, you understand that sitting in a boat fishing is an honest form of cardio vascular exercise.

Ifen, You understand that it is totally unfair for a female hunter or fisherperson to resort to crying when being checked by a game warden.

Ifen, you also understand that crying is a form of blackmail and will be treated as such.

Ifen, you understand that Yes & No are a perfectly acceptable answer to a question from a game warden and all questions answered with a "But aaaaW..." will be accepted as a No answer.

Ifen, you understand that subtle answers do not work, strong hints do not work, and beating around the bush will not work!

Ifen, you understand you only come to the game warden with a problem you want solved, that's what we do; sympathy is what you get from Wifee.

Ifen, your problem has been recurring every deer season for more then ten years you should maybe check with your doctor.

Ifen, we had this same conversation last year, and the year before, your excuse is inadmissible in this year's conversation. In fact after the second time around it becomes null and void.

Ifen, the conversation you are having with a game warden can be interpreted two ways, and one way makes you angry, guess which one the game warden meant.

Ifen, you ask the game warden to do something and then tell him how you want it done, you already know best how to do it, so just do it yourself and take your chances.

Ifen, you will understand that when talking with a game warden you are not doing a TV commercial, and there will be no disclaimers in the fine print on the bottom of the ticket.

Ifen, you understand it is almost impossible to get lost out in the woods, after all Christopher Columbus did not need directions.

Ifen, you understand that everyone has an itch somewhere they cannot reach to scratch and most hunting and fishing digest are written with this in mind.

Ifen, the game warden ask you, "what's wrong"? and you say "nothing" he will act like nothing is wrong, but know you are lying but some things are not worth the hassle.

Ifen, you ask a game warden a question you don't want to hear the answer too, expect an answer you don't want to hear.

Ifen, you ask a game warden what they are thinking be ready to discuss hunting, fishing, boating, snowmobiling, and other outdoor adventures.

Ifen, you are aware of the fact you already have enough hunting cloth to last a lifetime.

Ifen, you are aware of the fact you already have enough hunting boots when you can only wear one pair at a time.

Ifen, you understand that that the local game warden is in shape! Round **IS** a shape!

Ifen, you think after reading this you will better understand and be able to carry on an intelligent conversation with a game warden you had better take up golfing.

I was thinking the other day, as I was going over some bills, and this made my factitious mind kick into gear. The first of the following will surely tell what your age is.

Ifen, you can remember when your house payment was lower than your natural gas bill is now!

Ifen you can remember when your car payment was lower than your water bill is now!

Ifen, you can remember when you went out to shovel the driveway you actually shoveled the driveway using a shovel.

Ifen, you can remember when shoveling the driveway was such a project that the whole family had a hand in it.

Ifen, you can remember when the "snow scoop" came along and you thought this high tech improvement was a gift from heaven.

Ifen, you can remember when your favorite person was the man behind the wheel of the snowplow that filled in your driveway right after you got done "shoveling" it!

Ifen, you can remember when your feet were never warm from December until spring even with the good wool socks mom knit you!

Ifen, you can remember when at the first snow you could not get into a gas station and it had nothing to do with the price of gas, everybody was putting their snow tires on at the last minute.

Ifen, you can remember all the trouble it could be to start an old car with a choke in the below zero weather. (Not all new things are bad.)

Ifen, you went to bed under a paper mill blanket when the weather got really cold.

Ifen, your bedroom was only heated three months out of the year in the U.P.

Ifen, you can remember when your job was to bring the wood or coal in from the wood shed, in knee deep snow, in below zero weather, and it wasn't considered child abuse.

Ifen, you can remember when on a cold winter Saturday bath nights, you kept adding hot water to the same tub of water as you rotated the kids in and out according to age.

Ifen, the first time you had a shower was during gym class at school.

Ifen, one of your jobs was "shoveling" out under the clothes lines so mom could hang out the Monday wash so it could freeze dry.

Ifen, your first snowmachine was a Husky.

Ifen, one of the winter's big projects was watching the men cut ice squares from the river, when the ice got thick enough, and pack it in a shed of sawdust to keep it all through the summer. It was the first ice machine you ever saw in action.

Ifen, you can remember that one statement that could cause serious brain damage to a youth growing up in Yooperland it was when they lost their mittens that grandma knit for them. It went like this, "Well, where did you have them last!" And you thought, if I knew where I had them last I would walk back there and pick them up!

Ifen, you can remember when mom ask you to get something for supper out of the freezer, you went out to get it from the trunk of the old car out in the yard.

Ifen, you can remember when the nicest place in the house during the winter was the kitchen, when your Aunt was cooking with the wood cook stove in high gear.

Ifen, you can remember when you always tried to figure out how those using a wood cook stove could figure out how hot the oven was and how long it took things to cook.

Ifen, you can remember that one of the best smells in the world was when you came in the house on a cold winter day to smell those rutabagas cooking.

Just a few items for you that fall under the old fossil group to think about and remember back in the "Good Old Days".

Pre Game Warden Exam

So, you want to be a game warden! Well, here is a list of questions you have to be able to answer before you even get to first base in the long process.

So here is your pre-pre exam to see if you pass to take the real one.

1. Can you cry under Water?

2. Why do you have to "put in your two cents worth"... But it's only a "penny for your thoughts"? Where's that extra penny?

3. Once you're in heaven do you get stuck wearing the clothes you were buried in for all eternity?

4. Why does a round pizza come in a square box?

5. What disease did cured ham actually have?

6. How is it that we put a man on the moon before we figured out it would be a good idea to put wheels on luggage?

7. Why is it that people say they "slept like a baby" when babies wake up every two hours?

8. Why if a deaf person has to go to court is it still called a hearing?

9. Why is a person in the movie, but you're on TV?

10. Why do normal people pay to go up in tall buildings and then put money in binoculars to look at things on the ground?

11. Why does a doctor leave the room so you can change when they're going to see you naked anyway?

12. Why do toasters always have a setting that burns the toast to a horrible crisp, which no normal human being would eat?

13. Can a hearse carrying a corpse drive in the carpool lane?

14. If the "Exspurts" on Gilligan's Island can make a radio out of a coconut, why can't they fix a hole in a boat?

15. Why does Goofy stand erect while Pluto remains on all four? They are both dogs! Then how about Scooby Doo?

16. If Wiley E. Coyote had enough money to buy all those ACME traps to try and catch a road runner why didn't he just buy dinner?

17. If corn oil is made from corn, and vegetable oil is made from vegetables, what is baby oil made from?

18. Does the alphabet song and the Twinkle, Twinkle Little Star song have the same tune?

19. If you think you are qualified to be a game warden why did you just sing those two songs?

20. How did an asteroid and a hemorrhoid get their name?

So there you are twenty questions to see where you stand in the ranks of future game wardens.

Conservation Officer's Stories
Upper Michigan Tales from a Game Warden's Perspective
Some More Older Game Wardens

I guess I wanted you to get an idea and feeling for those game wardens that set a standard for those of us that would follow years later. If you take a minute and remember that I worked with a number of officers that replaced these I have told about in this book. In fact some of those I worked with came to work while some of these were still working.

Back in the "good old Days" it was nothing for game wardens to work well into their seventies. Personally I have to wonder how they ever did it with the conditions they had to work under. Needless to say when they were out working in the field they were on their own with no way to get any help even if it had been available, which in most cases it wasn't.

Besides please remember that I have always been a history nut that liked to read about how life used to be. If you stop and think about it and what people accomplished back then was pretty amazing.

You see I can remember when I was a youth growing up in the western U.P. in Ontonagon many a time the local game warden hooked a ride with us back to the "middle of no-where" to check on something because he had no way to get there. We either used a team of horses or a "bug" that someone had made. The officers back then drove their own cars so they were limited. When I started I had to drive my own vehicle until I was issued a patrol car.

In fact, I can recall when even some of the fire officers had to depend on local people to help get their fire fighting equipment back to a fire. For this reason some of the older relatives told me that when they were kids it was nothing to know where 3-4 forest fires were burning. Back then they just had to let them burn themselves out at times.

The following article was in the January, 1943 Michigan Conservation Magazine. It was written by Harry L. Aldrich, of Field Administration.

An Old Officer Explains

There is more to making a conservation officer than can be learned from books, or so one believes after hearing Conservation Officer Edward A. Deuell relate the history of his career in the department.

In April, 1914, a sturdy chap stamped with the mark of the rough north country came up to Bill Pearson, now Commissioner William H. Pearson of Boyne Falls, chief fire warden for the state Michigan, and said, "Bill, Why don't you give me a job fighting your fires?" The chap was Ed Deuell.

The state of Michigan had just began to take over the real job of handling forest fires from the various local and private agencies such as the Michigan Hardwood association which had a number of keymen and fire bosses scattered through the hardwood and hemlock areas of northern Michigan. Pearson had a real job to do and knew it. He lived in Boyne Falls in the heart of the big timber country and five miles from Ed Deuell's home. Harwood, hemlock, and pine slash had begun to cover the north. Great fires burned for days with inadequate equipment for their control. Settlers were rarely concerned until their homes and settlements were threatened. Fire laws were vague or unknown. Transportation was by logging spur, team or on foot. Pearson knew that Ed, at 42, had lived twenty or more of those years in the big timber. He knew that Ed had graduated from all four rooms of the Boyne City school at 17, that he had been a teamster in Chicago, a seaman on Lake Michigan, a fireman for the Union Pacific in Wyoming, a potential soldier in 1898 during the Spanish fracas, a mill hand and finally a railroad engineer on the B.G.& A. line, which Ed helped to build and of which Mr. Pearson is now president. He knew too that Ed blew a wicked slide trombone in the local band but never his own horn. Knowing all these things, he hired him on the spot.

Started as Fire Warden

It later developed that the new man also had his fair share of common variety of guts displayed in the north woods in those days and the ability to take it.

His first assignment was a logging spur ride into the Richardson Camp No.7 area which is the present site of the Pigeon river CCC camp about twenty miles east of Vanderbilt. During that summer of 1914, armed with his first commission as a state fire warden, Ed gained his first experience in state service and proved his worth to his employer.

That winter when deep snow came he was laid off but the spring of 1915 found him back with another assignment. This time he was sent to Sigma in Kalkaska county where he established an office. He found that his troubles had increased in that he also has become a game and fish warden with unlimited territory.

Ed says the going was tough with the only mans of travel a three-wheeled railroad velocipede borrowed from the Michigan Hardwood association. He kept this greased and his arms grew strong from pumping it over the myriad of logging sours that lined the country in those days.

A Squaw Holds the Fort

In 1929, Ed was transferred back to Charlevoix. He and Jake Smith, who had been appointed and stationed at Kalkaska, had a system all their own on trapping violations. They knew they couldn't catch all the trappers on the streams and lakes so they kept a list of those whom they suspected and each fall before the season opened, they made the rounds with search warrants when they could get them and without when they couldn't. They visited each trapper's house and searched, picked up many illegal pelts. On one occasion, they arrived at the home of a descendant of Chief Pontiac. The Chief himself was away but the squaw was very much in evidence. In those days they had string latches on the doors and when she saw them coming she pulled in the string so they couldn't get in. They finally forced the door and ed found himself looking right into a big fish spear wielded by the portly squaw. Ed objected to this so she dropped it and replaced it with a wicked skinning knife which she attempted to poke into his stomach. The boys beat a hasty retreat. Jake decided to go call the prosecuting attorney for advice while Ed stuck to his ground. About this time ED saw the Chief himself coming down the river

81

with a sack on his back and he ducked behind an out-house. When the Chief came along Ed stepped out and grabbed the sack and said, "What have you got there?" The Chief said, "Ugh! Porcupine for squaw." But it proved to be fresh rat and mink hides instead. Ed told him he has better make his squaw behave so he could look over the house. The Chief obligingly complied and ordered the squaw to desist and Ed proceeded to find another sack of illegal fur in the house. Then they proceeded to court in Kalkaska.

Becomes District Supervisor

He had many such adventures while in this area. In 1920 he was allowed to transfer back to his home county of Charlevoix. He had maintained his home in Boyne City and through the years had only been able to return once a week or so. Therefore, he was pleased to work out of his own home again. However in the winter this had its drawbacks in that there was no winter travel by car to speak of and he had to snowshoe many miles. He used to start from Boyne City on 'shoes and cover his area before returning, stopping over night at whatever village or farmhouse he could reach.

Ed worked his county as a game warden until 1924. By that time new laws had been enacted, the state had been divided up into different districts for better fire protection and for better law enforcement and Ed was picked to become the district supervisor in charge of one of those districts with headquarters in Boyne City. He now had a great many more things to do than the mere job of being a fire warden and stream policeman. Public sentiment toward conservation matters was changing rapidly and there were many more demands on the officer's time than heretofore. Ed was assigned a district of four counties, Charlevoix, Emmet, Cheboygan and Antrim. For the next six years, or until 1930, Ed proceeded to organize and supervise this district which at present is known as District 8.

Has Been Potent Force

All this time Ed was getting older. The physical rigors that he had withstood through his years of service were beginning to take their tool. New ideas and new methods and new phases of organization were being brought into the outfit by younger men and the portion as supervisor of a district no longer suited him. Therefore, in 1930, he was glad to turn the supervision of such matters over to others and take his old place as a conservation officer in Charlevoix county.

Ed Deuell has been a potent force in selling the public the importance of good conservation practices. He has had a way about him that has enabled him to be on friendly terms with practically everyone he has met, a way that has enabled him to make arrest and still remain friends with the persons he has arrested. It is a common occurrence today to accompany Ed Deuell on a trip through any of several counties and to find persons in every walk of life going out of their way to call, "Hello, Ed! Hello Ed! Where have you been?"

ED DEUELL

A boat load of walleye

Chapter 14

Conservation Officer's Stories **Upper Michigan Tales from a Game Warden's** **Perspective**

Bet You Didn't Know This

The famous Garden Peninsula south of Thompson has always been a rather interesting place for some of the activities that have taken place there. Some of the things the natives were involved in were those activities where rugged men were willing to battle the elements to earn a living. In today's world some of the money making schemes some people on the peninsula are involved in are of a different variety.

One of the programs on TV I enjoy watching is called *"The deadliest Catch"*. This is about commercial fishing up in the Bearing Sea. So this is a Yooper's version.

I came across the following article from 1943 by the education division of the Department of Conservation.

Michigan "Liberty Lobster"

With the submarine menace making lobster and shrimp rare and costly, the lowly fresh-water Michigan crab is becoming a delicacy on mid-western tables.

Catching crayfish, which every schoolboy who ever went near a swimming hole knows as crabs, is a business on the Garden Peninsula. Commercial fishermen on this narrow strip of land which separates Big Bay de Noc from Lake Michigan are doing their part to help solve the war-time food shortage by making these plebian cousins of the lobster and shrimp available for tables which have been bare of seafood during the war.

Prepared in the same manner as lobster and shrimp, crayfish are alleged to be delicious served in salads or on the shell.

These crayfish, never before considered anything more than a bathing beach pest or good bass bait, are trapped by commercial fishermen in box traps and shipped alive to distributors.

The traps are boxes made of ordinary lath 18 inches long, 8 inches wide, and 8 inches deep, with a small funnel in each end to enable the crayfish to enter. The lath is places about 1/2 inch apart to enable the small ones to escape, and to permit light to enter the trap so that the crayfish may see the bait that is placed inside. The top is removable to permit inspection of bait and removal of the catch. A piece of concrete in each end makes sure the box sinks to the bottom.

The bait usually consists of fresh fish-heads and must be changed daily, because the crayfish will not enter a trap that is baited with old meat or fish. The bait is suspended on a wire hook from the top of the trap. Lines of as many as 300 traps are set in about 5 to 30 feet of water. Each trap is marked by a float at the end of a length of quarter-inch rope.

Some fishermen use a rowboat to move along to lift their traps; some a motor boat, with the engine throttled to slow speed as the craft moves along the line of floats which are about 100 feet apart. While a man "gaffs" the floats with a hook and lifts the traps, the other removes the catch and rebaits the traps for resetting in another place. The catch may average about 15 crayfish per trap.

The smallest ones taken from the trap for shipment are 3 _ inches in length, and they usually range from 3 _ to 6 inches. An average day's yield from Garden Bay is about 2,000 crayfish.

They are sold by the hundred rather than by the pound, and will average about 16 to the pound, or about 6 pounds to the hundred. The fisherman takes great care to be sure that only live hard-shelled specimens are packed in the flat wooden boxes for shipping. Approximately 400 are shipped in each box.

Green Bay and Milwaukee are the main distributing points, and the market price is fairly consistent at $1.00 per hundred.

Boiled for about 10 minutes, the crayfish becomes red as a lobster, and many people declare tastes just as good – claws and all. And it is alleged that the severed tail where most of the meat is found is sweeter than shrimp or Japanese crabmeat, providing the diner is willing to fuss a bit with shell removal to find out.

Taking the crayfish commercially is not regulated by law, but the natural season for trapping them extends from about July 15 to October.

Unlike most types of commercial fishing intensive fishing tends to improve this branch of the industry, because the numerous small ones, which are always thrown back, feed well on the bait in the traps, and they grow faster and spawn quicker.

The following pictures are of crayfish fishermen on Garden Bay

Chapter 15
Conservation Officer's Stories
Upper Michigan Tales from a Game Warden's Perspective
Some That Got Away

It is amazing as you get older and older in life for some reason as you come across some of the adversaries you used to chase through the woods they for some reason like to tell you about how you almost caught them one time. Now most honest game wardens will be the first to tell you that they never caught them all. In fact they are well aware of the fact if the truth be told they caught a very small percentage of those that were out there breaking the law.

Here are a few tales of those that got away.

I Was All Ready to Give Up

If you have ever been involved in conservation law violations you soon are to realize that the hardest poachers to catch are those that do all their illegal activity in the back forty. If they never use a vehicle, never shine a light, never really leave their own property it makes catching them 90% luck and ten percent skill on the part of the old game warden.

In this story this was just one of those cases. It seems that the party involved did all his hunting on his own property. He very seldom left his property and if he was to go hunt somewhere else he was straight laced enough to be a choir boy. Therefore if he wanted to pop something for a little meat, all that he had to do was get it home into the barn and he was home free.

On this day he was going down a fence row on the back of the farm when an opportunity came along for a little freezer meat so he took it.

So when our opportunist is heading back home he all of a sudden realizes that just maybe things are not going as planned.

His thoughts went something like this; did you ever have one of those days when you figured you had reached the end of the road and finally life had caught up with you? This is a tale about someone who figured he was going to have a real bad day.

Remember, we started out with this hunter who was sitting out along a fence row not far from the house hoping his luck would change and he would finally get a nice buck.

This was not to be the case, so after a number of frustrating days he decided to get something to eat anyway. It is called freezer meat, which means it can be either legally or illegally taken. Usually the latter.

Finally something came in that was not quite legal, in fact it was not even close to being legal, but he shot it anyway. Just about the time he walked over to look at it he heard a helicopter come over the hill. Here he was standing out in the open, with his not to legal kill, with no place to hide. He figured the only thing he could do was to walk casually as he could back towards the house.

The helicopter circled over his house, then came right down the fence row, and passed right over him. He saw his whole life pass before his eyes and figured the law of average had finally caught up with him. As he walked into the yard, the helicopter passed over him and the house again, circled the field, and came back towards him.

This time it came over the house real low and he figured this is it because it landed right in the field between his place and the neighbor's house. As he stood there and watched figuring there was no use in trying to hide, some officers got out of the helicopter and ran up to the neighbor's house.

As our hunter standing there in a cold sweat was to find out later a couple of the neighbor's boys were growing pot back over the hill and that was the reason the helicopter was there.

It is totally amazing what a guilty consciences can do for you.

Within a Heart Beat

There are both advantages and disadvantages to driving along without any lights on. When you do this you hope everything you have planned works out just right so you can catch the poachers you are after.

On this night the game wardens had spotted a car using a spotlight in a field down the road from them. They took their time and worked their way to where they could ambush this vehicle at just the right time to catch those in it. It seemed to work out pretty good and they came up behind the vehicle without any lights on and all of a sudden turned on their headlights, their spotlights, and pulled up right behind the car using the light.

There were three guys in the car they had stopped, so they got out to check them out. They found the spotlight, a gun case and even some shells, but there was no sign of any firearm. They looked all over and even checked both side of the road and could not find anything.

Now it is not uncommon for a vehicle up here in the north woods to have shells and maybe even a gun case laying in them during the fall hunting seasons. But in this case, with the three that were in the car there was reason to believe that just maybe they should have had a gun. But the officers could not find one.

Years later I was at a funeral of one of the stars of my books where there were a group of old gray haired guys standing around telling stories. Now these old gray haired guys were this old game warden and some of those he chased around thirty years ago.

As we were reliving life one of them ask me if I remembered the time we had stopped a car shining over near the Philip's farm? He then told me the rest of the story and filled in the missing link.

It seems that just as we pulled up and hit our lights to check the car, this party had been standing outside the car near a big spruce tree. As all the patrol car lights came on he just dived under the spruce tree and laid on the gun he had. He never moved an inch all the time we checked the vehicle and the ditches on both sides of the road and we never knew he was there.

He then told me, "John, if you had just shut your car off there is no doubt you would have heard my heart beating because it was beating so hard I thought I was going to have a heart attack!"

Score on this one: poachers 1 - game wardens 0.

91

As the years fly by it seems that there are always new ways of breaking the law coming along that we would have never even imagined years ago. This is one of those areas.

In the area where I worked in the U.P. the judge I started out with was one of the few judges that I knew of that was a real outdoor person. He loved to hunt and fish and was well capable of doing some of the stupid things most sportsmen manage to do now and then. For this reason he was known to bring the hammer down on anyone that would take advantage of a person who had a camp or hunting and fishing equipment that you really couldn't protect from thieves.

But I do not think even this judge ever thought of what lay down the road.

I have written a number of times about the fact that some fishermen can have many thousands and thousands of dollars tied up in their fishing boats and gear. I guess it was only a matter of time before we would start reading about and hearing warnings about the theft from these boats. In the last little while I have heard a number of these stories.

You have to remember that in a lot of cases there is really no way to hide or protect all the gear you may have in your boat. Even the items that are attached can be quickly removed with a battery operated saw with a metal blade. With what some of the new gear, like I talked about really cost, it was only a matter of time before some low life would figure out how to steal it. Then with the yard sale craze all over the country you can even peddle it from these, along with all the second hand stores that are all over.

I also think that one of the easiest ways to get rid of items taken from hunting, fishing camp, or from a boat, is to peddle it on one of those on-line auctions. With this new way of fencing items they could end up almost anywhere in the country.

It was not by accident when I used the term to describe anyone that would steal out of someone's fishing boat, their deer blind, or ice fishing shanty as low life. In most cases there is just no way you can really make these places theft proof from someone wanting to steal from them. As we were taught in the army, "A padlock does not stop a thief it only keeps an honest person honest." It is the same way with our hunting and fishing gear we cannot take into the house or motel room with us.

Where have the days gone when a guys fishing boat, fishing shanty or deer blind was safe from thieves? I can remember when deer rifles were left in unlocked deer blinds on public land. There were unlocked ice fishing shanties, full of gear ready for the next trip out on the lake. You could pull your fishing boat up on the landing and leave it there ready for an early start in the morning, but you sure take a chance in this day and age if you do this now.

So this is just a word of warning! Beware about the changing times some of you that have your fishing boat all decked out with the latest toys. Beware!

The Game Warden Should Know a Track

I have always told my kids when they were little that, "Game Wardens know everything." And for a few years they maybe even believed it. You have to read this story to realize what it can lead to.

I have to tell this story because all of you grandpa's out there will understand just what took place. You see grandpa's have special rights when it comes to grandkids. What they do and what they say just makes sense to those little guys.

My grandson who lives in Florida and is in kindergarten is a dinosaur nut! This little guy knows the names of the entire dinosaur family, which ones were meat eaters and the ones that were vegetarians. He has models and books of all these old timers.

When we were down there we went out to eat one evening when our projects were done. Upon finishing our meal and returning home grandma and grandpa took our two grandsons, the kindergartener and his cousin a year younger. As we were coming down the three miles of sand road towards my daughters house these two little guys were sitting in the back seat talking about meat eating dinosaurs. I mean there was some serious discussion going on.

93

All of a sudden grandpa stopped the car and told the two little guys to get out of their seat belts because it looked like dinosaur tracks going down the road in front of us!

(Now you have to understand that when we went to town a few hours before we had passed some people riding horses in this area.)

The two little guys jumped up looked out the front window and sure enough there were tracks going down the road. And to top it off it looked like it may have been a mother with a little one tagging along behind! Of course grandpa was quick to point out this fact for them. We were really lucky because it seems these dinosaurs must have turned off before they got to their house, but in their mind there was no doubt what made the tracks!

The end of the story? Not really.

Monday evening my daughter called and said, "Thanks a lot dad!" It seems she was returning home after picking up the boys. They were going along this same sand road when all of a sudden the boys started yelling, "Roll up the windows Mom! Quick roll up the windows!"

She had no idea what was going on so she quickly rolled up the windows and asked Zack what it the world was wrong? He was quick to inform his Mom that there were more dinosaur tracks going right down the middle of the road!

O' the fun of being a grandpa.

In the many, many miles I have traveled both in my job as a game warden and later in life with my books I got to meet some unusual people. In this chapter I would like to tell you about some of these people and organizations.

I have always said that if there is an outstanding organization somewhere there are outstanding people involved that make it work as you will see here.

Kingsley's Outdoor Adventure Club

One weekend I was down in Traverse City at an Outdoor Show and had the best weekend of any with my books. I guess one of the main reasons was that Ron Jolly who has the morning talk program on 580 WTCM had me on the morning before the show started. We talked about my books and what they were like and I told some stories. We also talked about the scholarship fund so people would know about it. I tried to keep track of all the people that came up to my booth at the show and told me they heard the Ron Jolly program. But it got so busy on Saturday after counting 75 people that I lost count. Besides for a Yooper you were getting up into big numbers. What a great weekend and I'm thankful for people like Ron Jolly that are willing to help me out.

You know you always hear on the news, stories about messed up youth and about schools, who a lot of people blame for these problems. You begin to wonder if there is anyone out there trying to make a difference anymore. But then it seems that the good Lord sends something your way to once again provide a spark of what people that really care can do to try and change things. That is what took place this week.

You all know that I spent most of my life being involved with youth both as part of my job and through the church I attended, so I am always interested in what youth are doing. This past weekend down in Traverse City there was a booth from the Outdoor Adventure Club from Kingsley High School set up. All weekend long this booth was manned by youth that are part of this program selling raffle tickets for their upcoming project. What a great bunch of well mannered sharp looking young people they were. The ODAC (Outdoor Adventure Club) was founded in 1999 with 12 members and now it has over 70 members. The clubs goals are: (1)-Introduce kids to the outdoors in a positive way. (2)-Create an appreciation for the outdoors. (3)- Appeal to a wide variety of kids. (4)- Provide lifetime experiences. (5)- **Have fun!**

Their brochure states: Widening student's horizons and opening doors to a world around them is key to any school experiences. ODAC creates lifelong appreciations for our great outdoors. Here are some of the places and activities they raised money for and traveled to. Yellowstone National Park, The Badlands, Whitewater Rafting, Camping at the Porcupine Mountains on a camping trip and canoeing the Boundary Waters are some the places they have enjoyed. This year the group is raising money for a trip up to Alaska. Needless to say the youth are excited about this trip. I might add who wouldn't be!

What a wonderful program Kingsley High School has for their students, but it wouldn't be possible if some people didn't care about their future. I spent time talking to Matt Stevenson who works with these kids and saw his heart for the program. I also spent some time talking to the school principal that was there for the kids from his school all three days. There were other advisors and helpers there too and needless to say you could not have the successful type program they have without people being willing to sacrifice for the kids. The principal told me that a program like this was a God send for both the students and himself it was such a positive program.

So next time you hear on the news all the negative problems out there with today's kids remember there are always those scattered around making a difference as best they can like the students and staff people of the Outdoor Adventure Club. You will also see if you are an old fossil like me that there is still hope for our nation because of these young people and programs like this.

I had more fun with all these young people and needless to say it made the weekend well spent. You can find out more about Kingsley High School by just typing their name in on Google.

I was later to be the speaker at the Outdoor Adventures Club Big Buck Night and had a great time. Not only this but I was able to be there with a hunter that actually shot an official 30-point buck. His story is next.

Honest! A Thirty Point Buck

I spoke at the Kingsley's banquet and this man was there.

Could you not picture this party calling home and trying to convince those there that he had shot a 30-point buck?

As I understand the story a family member had purchased a hunting trip and could not go. He offered it to Ron, but he was not really interested. He got talked into going only to get there and then being told how bad the hunting was where he would be sitting.

So here he is where he didn't plan on being, sitting in a place where there were no deer, only to have this buck walk in.

Checking out the commercial walleye catch pictured on page 84. This was one of the worse jobs a game warden ran into.

Chapter 17

Conservation Officer's Stories **Upper Michigan Tales from a Game Warden's** **Perspective**

An Old Game Warden's Philosophy on Life

Needless to say times are really different from when I first put on the Conservation Officer's uniform. When I started you were still learning from the "Old school" officers that had fought in the big war and had a whole different prospective on life, liberty, and family. As I have stated before, when I was interviewed for the job as a Michigan Conservation Officer, they not only interviewed me but Wifee also. Back then it was considered a team effort and your wife was to be part of the team seeing you worked out of your house and she was the one usually home answering the phone and talking to people that came by. Back then you even sold trapping license from your home. Now days it is a whole new ball game with different players and different rules.

In this chapter I would like to talk about some of the changes I have observed and my personal opinion on them, which may not be worth a whole lot to anyone but myself.

Now each of these points I have talked over with my dog out at camp and he seems to agree with each one providing I give him a treat after discussing each one.

Change in Duties

Back in the "olden" days it was required that the game warden attend the meetings and activities of the local sportsmen's clubs. It did not matter if and when they were you were just expected to be there. There was a two-fold reason for this: First it was so you would get to know the local sportsmen and build a bond with them so they would feel they could call you if they ran across something in their outdoor travels. It was just felt that you were more likely to get a call from someone who could put a face to the local game warden than them just calling an 800 number. It seemed to work too.

The second reason, needless to say, there were times when things came up that they would like to ask you about. It was felt by the then Conservation Department that it was part of your duties to make yourself available to these groups. I do have to say that in almost all cases where I was assigned to work that these sportsmen's groups were an important part of my success.

Needless to say they may not have always agreed with the direction that the department was taking, but I cannot recall them ever taking it out personally on me.

Now many, many years later I will still run into members of some of these clubs that will come up to me as a friend and recall old times we had together at these meeting. It was time well spent.

Speaking of Time Well Spent

Of course you have to remember that back in the so called "good old days" you did not work in hours. In fact on your time sheet you did not even mark down the hours you worked. If it was a work day you marked it with an X to show you worked on that day. It did not matter if you had put in 3 hours or had worked 18 hours on a project. It was just shown as a X for a work day. This math I could handle.

If you were off for a day you were to show this day as a P on your work sheet. It meant you were on pass that day and had not worked at all. If you had planned to take a day off and a call came in about some poaching taking place you were expected to go out and check on it. It went with the job you had hired on to do.

The biggest change that has taken place is that from the first of October, when hunting season really got started, until the middle of December you basically never got a day off. It was felt that this was when the sportsmen paying the bills expected the game warden to be working so you had too. There was a period during the spring fish runs that were the same way that meant no days off.

Later on there was a change where you did keep track of hours and you were given comp time for all the extra hours you worked. I have to admit personally that I enjoyed this way of doing things. With the area I worked along Saginaw Bay I would have enough comp time that along with my normal vacation I could take two long vacations. I would spend a three-four week period each year with Wifee's family down in Missouri and also a three-four weeks with my parents up in Ontonagon.

You work long steady hours at times, but you felt you were rewarded with the family time later on.

But needless to say things changed through the years.

Now Ruled By Success

As I have referred to before when I started there were still a lot of the "Old School" around. These were the guys that worked out in the field for their whole career as a game warden. Some of these men spent 30-40-and a few 50 years out in the field working as a conservation officer. Most of them worked right up to seventy years of age when they had to retire.

But these old timers never had any real ambition to climb that ladder and try to reach the top of the mountain. In fact, I knew a number of them that were talked into making that jump up the ladder only to give it up a short time later and come back to work in the field.

In so many cases today this is not the case. From the day some of these new officers start working their goal is to reach the top of the mountain and rule the roost.

When this is the case I have seen that their whole perspective on life is different than those that love the job as a field officer.

You have to admit that there are not too many rungs in the ladder of success by serving the people of a one-horse U.P. town out in the middle of no-where. In fact the only time those in the "big-house" realize you are still around is when you manage to "screw-up" again. I use the word again because needless to say I have been there.

One time I went to pull someone out of a snow bank while on patrol. I had hooked up to their vehicle and onto the trailer hitch ball on mine. I did manage to pull them out but when I walked to the back of my patrol vehicle the bumper had been deformed. What had been a nice straight bumper now was shaped in a perfect V.

I tried to justify this by saying we should really have our vehicles come with a better trailer hitch, but it fell on deaf ears.

Then there was the time I was requested to be in Lansing for an interview for a promotion down in the Detroit area. Now understand I was not asked, but requested to attend. I was not even asked if I was interested in the job in the first place, I think they just needed another body to talk too.

So down I went and would you believe it the night before I was to attend this interview with the powers to be in the "big house" I realized I had left in such a hurry I had forgotten to bring any shoes but the old, beaten up tennis I had on! What now!

So being a normal, red-blooded, Yooper I decided to do the only thing I could, go out and buy some shoes to wear to the meeting I never wanted to be at in the first place.

About the time I got home I received a call from my boss that there had been a complaint that my patrol car had been spotted in a Myer's parking lot in Lansing and the powers in being wanted to know what it was doing there!

Now what's wrong with this picture? First of all, these same powers in being asked me to be in Lansing to attend a meeting I never wanted to be at in the first place. Second could they not figure that just maybe the reason a patrol car from the U.P. was in Lansing was because they asked it and me to be there?

But to justify things I had to sit down and write a letter explaining just why I was down at the "big house" to see the same people that ask me to come. Of course I could not tell them what was really on my mind because I wanted them to forget me and let me return to the safety of the U.P. as soon as possible.

Sometimes even a good U.P. boy has trouble staying hidden and being satisfied with working in the field.

Old Fences Torn Down

It seems as more and more time goes by that the new generation has somehow come up with better ideas as to how to save the world. It does not matter that so many of the "Old School"

102

throughout the Conservation Department-DNR had dedicated their whole life to just doing that very thing.

I have written before that if laws (that had been on the books for decades) against polluting our water-ways had been enforced like they should have been half the problems we have today would not have happened. But the problem has never really been the men in the field, but the lawyers and politicians that come into play. Needless to say the guy working out in the field, on the front lines, cannot fight city hall so to speak.

The other area where the fences have been moved is where some of the laws that have been on the books for years are suddenly being re-interrupted by the new generation in the "big house". Now you have to understand that laws are supposed to be passed to control a problem that our legislators in their wisdom saw as needing fixing.

So here is an area where there is a need for some enforcement to protect our natural resources, so a law to address this problem at the time is passed. But now umpteen years later the powers in being in the "big house" look at this same law and re-interrupt the reason for it and how it should be enforced.

One of the best examples of the evolution of a law I think I can address is the uncased gun law. This law was passed to try and stop road hunters when there were a lot of pheasants in Lower Michigan, and those that feel that a deer blind comes with 4-wheels and a motor. In other words it was meant to stop road hunters.

When I started out as a game warden the law was there on uncased firearms in a motor vehicle. Now remember there were not 4-wheelers as are used in hunting today. At that time the enforcement policy for uncased firearms read: "*Enforcement action will be taken only when there is an overt act of hunting from a motor vehicle.*"

Back then we did not enforce the uncased gun law unless there were other factors involved. But I saw the enforcement of this law change from this to where if they had an uncased gun at all in a motor vehicle a ticket was issued. Remember back then if they had the bolt out of a bolt action, or the gun was broke down, they did not have to have it in a case.

Then I saw it evolve to where if the firearm was not completely in a case, enforcement action was taken. In other words even if the firearm was in the back seat, in a case, but the zipper was maybe unzipped a couple of inches a ticket was issued.

The whole attitude towards those out hunting went from using a law to catch the bad guys like it was meant to be, to catch anyone who may have a case partly zipped but had no intention of hunting from his vehicle.

This is not the only law where I could point out that the "old fences" or parameters were pushed aside and a whole new way of enforcing the law was taken.

Are they technically breaking the law, yes, but is it a wise and prudent law enforcement action, one wonders.

Use of Exspurts

I guess there has always been a problem where what some people have to say outweighs what others may have to say, but I think in today's world things have went too far towards one side.

It used to be, that a person that spent a lifetime in the great outdoors and been involved in some hunting, fishing, and trapping activities felt he had learned something, and that he had a honest opinion on what he felt should be done to improve these activities. But today most of these people feel it is a waste of time to even try and speak at the meetings held around the state.

I will again give you an example. In the area where I was working there were some brothers that had trapped for years. They were real successful in taking almost every type of fur bearer out there. What got my attention about these brothers was the fact that they had kept a yearly diary for more than forty years of what they had caught, where they had caught it, the type of season it had been, and the quality of the fur.

If you were to read one of their diaries you would be able to see what the fall and spring trapping season weather conditions were. Snow or lack of it, water depth and the spring thaw, how many beaver or other fur bearers they removed from each dam, and what quality the hides were in and what they brought at the fur sale.

If you were to take a forty year spread of all this information you could come up with some rather interesting facts on fur harvesting for the three-county area I was stationed in.

One time when we were having a meeting on fur trapping with some biologist I mentioned to them that they should go by and see some of these yearly books these brothers had kept all these years.

They were interested until they found out that these brothers were just some average back-woods boys that had not even finished high school. They had worked in the woods most of their life and had never cared to venture very far from home.

So with the background of these brothers the dairies were written off as useless because they were not college educated "Exspurts" in the area of trapping. I have observed this so many times in my dealings with those involved with the powers in being of the DNR.

In fact, while attending an annual bear hunters meeting I asked the head (at the time) of the Natural Resources Commission about the fact that they had formed a special committee to study the outdoor activities of Michigan and there was not one from the U.P. on it. I was told by him, "We do not care what the people from the U.P. think!" I was floored.

Later I wrote about this in a Fish Report and had calls and letters from all over saying that this attitude is exactly what's wrong with the DNR today.

Special Interest Groups

Needless to say, in all the years that I worked and even those years since I retired, being involved with the system that governs government one gets well aware of the special interest groups that control things.

Now please understand that almost all of these groups have an agenda to promote, which is the reason they were started in the first place. It is no secret that a group of people with a title are more apt to be heard than Joe and his buddy from Ontonagon. So

105

they form a club to push their ideas. Now a lot of these are started out with the best of intentions by a group of average people. But! As their influence and success grows they soon forget their roots and those average outdoor lovers that first organized the club.

Influence and success, sitting at the head table, and rubbing shoulders with the powers in being can have a startling influence on the best of people. If you don't believe me, look at Lansing and Washington where you see it happen all the time.

So what happens, pretty soon the input and ideas of the little guy carry no weight at all, and only those of a special interest group are considered. I have seen this first hand where the DNR would call a meeting to get the input of the "average hunter" on what they think. After spending time talking to these "average hunters" the meeting will close and the people from the DNR will go back into the corner of the room and meet with the special interest people and usually cancel out all they heard from the "average hunter".

Here again I will give you an example of how this works. Years ago the biggest special interest group in Michigan wanted a big game animal to promote as trophy animal in Michigan. Now understand here in Michigan your choices are few because unlike some states out west there are only so many animals that fit into this category. So the Exspurts decided on the black bear.

This is how the bear permit system came about. This special interest group did not want it so you could just walk in and purchase a bear license like had been the case for so many years. They felt you would feel like it was something special if you earn the right to hunt for black bear and had to wait years before your chance came.

They sure got their wish because sometimes those that enjoyed the fellowship and the camp life of the bear hunting season are lucky to get to hunt once every five to eight years.

The sportsmen were told one thing about how the system would be set up and then the DNR turned around and did something different in the way the points and drawings were to be run.

Then they went and made the areas with the influence of some special interest groups that wanted the boundaries set a certain way to take advantage of their style of hunting. Throughout the years that the permit system has been in affect hunters have tried to convince the Natural Resource Commission to cut Newberry Area in half but it falls on deaf ears because special interest groups want it left the way it is.

This is the reason one area covers almost half the U.P. while the other half is divided into a number of areas. Why? Influence of these special interest groups.

This also is the reason you are getting less and less of the average sportsmen that even both to attend DNR meetings that are held for public input. It is felt by many, "Why go, they never listen to us anyway?"

Of course this does not help the problem either.

Just a Job

It is interesting as I was writing this section of this chapter I came across an article on the internet by Dan Nephin of the Associated Press with the headlines: *State short on fish, game wardens.* It fits right into what I am saying in this chapter.

When I hired in as a game warden more than 3,500 people took a test hoping to land one of about 35 jobs for a career as a Michigan Conservation Officer. Back then it was not just taking a job for the sake of landing a job because the pay was not great and the hours were long, dark, and cold in a lot of cases. But you wanted to be one of those few people that maybe could have an affect on our natural resources protection.

The pay and benefits were not as good as most other law enforcement agencies and in fact the retirement was totally out of whack. In most cases forty years later it is no better.

This is why in so many cases today the game wardens you may meet out in the field are not from the "old school" of dedicated outdoor enthusiast that love the hunting, fishing, and natural enjoyments connected with them. In fact if the truth be known you may well run into a game warden today that never hunted or fished in their life. It may be the case that someone marked the box on the civil service exam for any job they qualified for and the game warden job is the one that came up.

107

There is another side to the story too. Back when I started law enforcement had their defined areas of responsibility. The game warden enforced fish and game laws, forestry laws, state parks and other laws pertaining to recreational use of the great outdoors.

Would you believe the game warden did not enforce the Marine Safety Act? This was enforced by the sheriff departments who were paid to do this. The game warden did not enforce Motor Vehicle Law violations. This was handled by the other law enforcement agencies within the counties they were assigned too.

On the other hand they did not enforce the Conservation Law violations but called out the local game warden to handle these. This did not mean that there was no cooperation between agencies when one was called on to assist another.

But in today's world the game warden may spend more time looking for and assisting in everything from drug enforcement to traffic stops than working Conservation Law violations.

In some states about 1/3 of the tickets written by game wardens are for other than Conservation Law violations. This may be one of the key reasons they cannot find people that want to be game wardens. Not traffic cops. In one state where only a few years ago they would have over 6,000 applicants for a game warden exam the last time out they had only a couple of hundred apply.

Back in the "good old days" even if the pay and retirement benefits were sub-par the reason for doing the job outweighed these shortcomings. But why take the job today if you are just going to be a traffic cop in a different colored uniform?

My Way-Only Way

Last, let me say that this here may be one of the key reasons why the job and the feelings for it has changed so much. Back in the good old days a game warden actually felt like he could make a difference out there. Not Today!

We can blame most of this on the fact that the biggest predator out there has gotten way out of hand. (I could write a whole book on my feelings about this problem throughout our nation.) This predator has made it so that the game warden out in the field cannot use his own judgment in most cases.

It used to be if you were called out to check on something you were expected to "use your head" and apply common sense judgment in how you handled the violation. But not now, it seems that everything has to fall into a black and white world. In so many cases you are flat told by those in the "big house" that you are out there to enforce the laws as they in the "big house" see fit. You are no longer allowed to apply your common sense to a case.

It boils down to the old adage, "It's our way-the only way" or should I say, "It's our gate and our fence and we tell you how to swing on it". I feel this is one thing that has hurt the game warden out in the field dealing with the public. All cases have circumstances that may influence how the game warden calls them.

In a lot of areas that modern day predator has played a big factor in how things are done. It was never the intent of our forefathers that the whole country be run by lawyers!

It was never the intent of our forefathers that both the senate, and the house, and even the president's office be almost totally controlled by lawyers. Would you believe that in our constitution it does not require that a judge on our Supreme Court be a lawyer? They, the lawyers, through their power in the system have caused this to take place.

This has filtered down to where the game warden working out in the field dealing with you cannot use common sense or his opinion on how to handle a violation because some lawyer may not like what he did and file a law suit over it. Then who does this suit go to but his lawyer buddy who is the judge. Would you believe when I started 99% of the tickets you wrote never went before a judge-lawyer, but before a Justice of the Peace who was just an average guy from the committee almost never being a lawyer.

But then it seems that there were a lot of lawyers out there looking for work so they created a job to keep them off of welfare. This is how the District Judge position came into being with Michigan's new constitution.

109

You can bet that most of these never hunted or fished a day in their life. In fact, in some of my other books I wrote about some of the things I came across in court.

So here we are today, you have to remember that when you come across a game warden and wonder why he acted the way he did, that he just maybe did not have any choice. In a lot of cases his mind was already made up for him before he even came across you out in the field.

I leave you with this question at the end of this chapter "What are our chances that things are going to get any better for the hunter, fisherman, and gun owner out there?"

During the course of my career there were a number of things that happened that left me scratching my head. There was no way that I personally could have ever taken a chance like some people I knew did. Maybe they were from the era when it was just a way of life, but for me forget it.

My Missing Canoe

You have to understand that when working as a game warden you are issued all kinds of toys to play with along with other equipment needed to do the job. When an officer has a number of boats, snowmobiles, ORV, trailers for each piece of equipment, plus everything you need to use, you are responsible for a ton of stuff.

When I worked in Tuscola County we had a waterfowl refuge on Saginaw Bay, state game areas, state parks, besides the normal areas where officers went on patrol. For this reason once a year at inventory time it was fun and games to try and locate all this equipment which was spread over a three-four county area in some cases. Everything that had a certain value had what was called a DA tag with number on it. Each year you would receive a computer print-out with all these DA numbers and a definition of what this tag should be on.

So off you would go trying to verify that the equipment was still around.

One year after a mentally challenging period I managed to find all the equipment on the list but one piece. Look as I might I could not find this 16 foot aluminum canoe. I looked in every state owned building in the three county area. I tried to get hold of anyone I thought might have used this canoe. No matter who I called or where I looked I could not find it.

After putting two and two together I finally figured out that the last place the canoe had been used was to patrol the marshes along

Saginaw Bay. After the waterfowl season the canoe was put up on the rafters in the Fish Point Refuge garage.

So I headed up to Fish Point to double check and make sure it was not tucked away somewhere up there. No luck, no canoe.

I finally figured I had looked everywhere the canoe could have been and mentioned at coffee one morning at the field office that I was going to have to file a report at the sheriff's office that this state canoe had been stolen.

All of a sudden a voice from down the table said, "You may want to wait a little while before filing that report, for I have a feeling in about a week your missing canoe will no longer be missing. In fact, it will be back up in the rafters at Fish point."

Now, how many miles and how many hours had I spent looking for this canoe, when there were people in the office all the time that knew where it was.

In fact, the canoe that I was responsible for was no longer located in the United States! In fact this law division canoe was no longer in the hands of law enforcement personal. In fact this canoe was now located in Canada on a moose hunting trip with some people out of the Lansing office.

Sure enough about a week later the canoe managed to find its way back up on the rafters in the Fish Point garage. Was I a happy camper over what had happened? Not really but strange things happen when there is a full moon.

Interesting What One Could Use It For

As I stated before when I first worked as a game warden you drove your own vehicle and were paid a monthly fee to cover the cost of doing this. So for almost all their career it did not matter what extra-curricular activities the old timers used their patrol vehicle for seeing it was theirs.

For some of the old timers it was hard after so many years to adapt to this new way of life. For this reason there were some of those that had to come up with a way to kill two birds with one stone.

There was this one old-timer that had always made it a point while out on patrol during the fall of the year to cut some firewood to take home. Why, it only made good since when you were already out in the woods if you saw a blow-down that would make some excellent firewood to get the chain saw out and cut it up. Then throw it in the back of your personal-patrol vehicle and haul it home. The big problem was now you were driving a marked, state owned, patrol car. So it was only common sense to figure that some people might not be impressed if they saw a marked, state owned vehicle hauling a trailer load of firewood home.

So this old timer came up with a way to solve this little problem. It seems that if he removed the complete back seat from his state owned patrol vehicle he could haul quite a bit of firewood home while out on patrol. (It works best if you have a 4-door vehicle.)

Things were going on pretty good, and had been for quite a while, until he was attending a district meeting and some of the powers in being decided to ride to lunch in his patrol car. They were needless to say surprised when they discovered that this was the only patrol car in the state without a back seat, and a floor covered with bark and sawdust.

....

Then there was the old timer that had always figured it was a good way to wind down after a hard day out in the field to stop off at the local golf club on the way home. No problem, when you were driving your own vehicle.

But along with the change to a state owned vehicle came a need to improvise. Seeing he couldn't very well park his marked, state owned patrol car in front of the 19th hole at the golf course he came up with a plan. It seems that a friend he golfed with lived right next to the golf course so he would park at his place either in his garage or behind his house. He would then change and get his clubs out of the trunk and walk out on the golf course.

Everything went great and he had been doing this for years. Then came the time when his patrol car had enough miles on it that it had to be turned in at the state motor pool in Lansing. A couple of days before he was to travel to Lansing to turn it in he cleaned out the car and got everything ready.

113

Off he went to Lansing, turned in his old patrol car. He picked up a new vehicle and headed home. Seeing it was not too late in the afternoon when he got near home, Lansing was right around 100 miles from his home, he decided to stop by the golf course.

He pulled into his buddy's yard and went to get his golf clubs out of the trunk of his patrol car. Only when the trunk came open he realized he had a problem.

Off he took over to the golf course and asked if it would be all right if he used their phone? He called one of his old time buddies that worked in the Lansing office and told him, "Get down to the motor pool as fast as you can and get my golf clubs out of the vehicle I just turned in!

Can I Borrow One

During all the years I worked as a game warden you felt you had heard and seen just about everything. But about the time you had thought there was nothing else left to surprise you along came a new one. Now maybe I was just naive but some things just never crossed my mind.

I was sitting at home one evening in late summer when I received a phone call from an officer who worked down state. I had never worked with this officer, but knew him from attending schools and training sessions.

He told me that he was coming up to the U.P. for a vacation in a couple of weeks and was wondering if there was a state boat at the Thompson field office he could use so they could do a little fishing.

Now he was not asking me if I had a boat he could use, but was asking if he could use one of the boats assigned to the officers working out of Thompson.

I sat there for a few minutes rather dumb founded because needless to say in over twenty years of service I had never run into this before. It was something I personally would have never thought to ask another officer so my silence must have answered his question for him.

We talked for a few minutes and then that was the end of things. To this day I have no idea if this was a common practice or if someone was just taking a shot in the dark trying to see what my answer would be.

Yard Sales

But the boating tale above is not the strangest thing I have run into in my travels as a game warden. As anyone could understand, when you have a job like I had you are issued a ton of equipment to use in the zillion of different things you are involved in.

As times goes on and things change a lot of these items are either replaced or have become outdated with a better piece of equipment in which to do the job.

In most cases the older gadgets are either collecting dust somewhere or are turned back into the district office.

Then there is all the items you come across while working out in the field. For example, if you come through the woods and a party is fishing without a license and he sees you before you can come up to him, chances are all that you will see is a thrown fishing pole and flying tennis shoes going off through the woods. So if you can't catch him you go back up and pick up the gear he had left behind.

I would then take the gear and place a tag on it and place it in the evidence locker just in case the party should come looking for it. Needless to say in all my years I never had anyone wanting their gear back bad enough to want a ticket to get it.

As time would go on you would end up having dozens of fishing poles and other pieces of outdoor gear sitting in the back room at the office. When enough time had passed I would call an organization like the Big Brothers and ask them if they would be interested in having some fishing poles and such. Needless to say they were more than happy to get these to use to take kids fishing. But I was to find out that some people had their ways of getting rid of old equipment they had and items they came across while working the field.

One day, after I had retired, I was running around the U.P. when I came across a place where they were having a yard sale. Me,

115

being a yard sale junkie pulled in to see what they had. To my surprise the person having the yard sale was a game warden I had known. He was not at home, but his wife and kids were having the yard sale.

Even more surprising as I looked around to see what he was peddling I saw more than one item that had been issued to work the field with. In fact, I am not sure I could not have re-equipped a patrol car with the things that were for sale.

Maybe a guy born in a place like Ontonagon grew up with a narrow vision of what you should do in life. In fact you older people will know what I am talking about when I tell this.

When I was working down state we purchased our gas for the patrol car from the regular gas stations in town. Back then, and this will age me, if you bought gas you could collect S&H green stamps with every purchase. Needless to say with all the miles we put on and the amount of gas we bought you could fill out a number of these green stamp books.

Me, being like I was I never took the stamps for the gas I purchased with the state credit card. I'm not saying if it was right or wrong to take them, I am just saying I didn't feel right taking them. So the station owner worked out a deal so he would fill out the booklets with stamps and then give them to a kids group who in turn could cash them in for outdoor equipment they could use.

I am not saying what is right or wrong, each person has to decide for themselves, but I made a lot of friends by handling things this way.

116

Conservation Officer's Stories
Upper Michigan Tales from a Game Warden's Perspective
Eino and Teivo Ride Again

If you are a true Yooper you will understand just who Eino and Teivo are. They are the fictional characters that seem to be able to understand some things that happen in the "Big House" better than those that are there.

Up here in God's Country, where people have grown up being able to see the big picture of life without first running it through a computer or having the "Exspurts" analyze it to figure out just how to do it, Eino and Teivo bring some common sense into ones life.

A New Thunder Tube

Before getting into this tale I have to say that true Yoopers have a real problem with being forced fed the things Washington and Lansing dream up. Sometimes some of their ideas would not pass the outhouse test. In other words to the average Yooper their justification for what they are doing stinks.

Eino and Teivo were reading the local weekly newspaper and came to realize just what they had missed out on. In fact neither of those two guys or the local game warden ever realized that Iron Creek was such a prolific trout stream. Eino had to admit this had to be one of the better kept secrets ever to come out of Washington.

This and the fact that there might be such a flood that it would wash out Thunder Lake Road! Teivo was of the belief that they must mean when the polar ice cap melts and all that water comes south down Iron Creek.

Eino says the even more amazing thing about the way those fellows operate out of Washington is the fact that this flash flood out of the Cooks Mountains to wash out Thunder Lake Road must be something new. Because they just resurfaced this road a few years ago so why didn't they do everything at once and replace the tube then.

So Teivo had to explain to him that the government doesn't work like this because it would make too much sense to the average person. Teivo went on to explain that all these Exspurts" who make all these plans maybe never tried to walk up or down Iron Creek or maybe they just did their walking on a computer.

Of course you have to understand that it has always been a mystery whenever someone caught a nice trout out in Indian Lake as to just where this trout had come from. I have to admit I heard a lot of theories, but not once did I ever guess, or hear anyone else guess that this trout may have come out of Iron Creek. I have to admit after all these years one can still learn something new when they take time to read the local paper.

Eino has been doing a lot of research into the best spawning grounds for brook trout after reading this article and figured he just maybe learned something new.

Eino and Teivo were always of the understanding that brook trout liked cool, clear water, just maybe with a little currant to it. But now they figure that the Exspurts must have come up with a new specie that likes tag alder marshes better than cool, clear, creeks with a sandy-gravel bottom.

Teivo thinks that the real disaster is going to come when Eino goes into this area to brook trout fish and tries to use his fly rod to float a few flies through a hole trying to hook a monster brook trout. Now that is problem one, number two is you are in the middle of a tag alder jungle so just how are you going to play this monster.

But look on the bright side, there is no red, blooded Yooper game warden that would ever think of coming along through this tag alder marsh to check and see if you have a trout stamp on your fishing license.

What's A True Yooper Really Worth

Eino ran into something the other day that really makes a guy wonder how much he is really worth. Maybe that is not the right way to word it, maybe he should say what I saw makes a guy realize how little he is worth.

A few days ago Eino and Teivo were driving some of the back roads from Munising to Manistique. When they were out in the middle of no-where they saw a sign that said "garage sale" and were hooked. First of all garage sales out in the middle of no-where can be a gold mine. And two, after seeing this sign they drive another five miles farther back into the middle of no-where.

They came up to this garage with its doors open where the sale was. They looked around and found nothing that they wanted, so much for that gold mine. Then the lady told them that the lady up on the hill was having a sale too. She said this lady had lost her husband last winter and was selling some items at a garage sale so they walked over.

In this garage they found a number of hunting items, a lot of outdoor books, and some duck carvings he had been working on. They looked the things over and Eino purchased a number of books and some carvings. They looked at some of his hunting clothes but the sizes were wrong for them.

After they left and were trying to get back to somewhere from the middle of no-where they got to thinking. For these two this can be a dangerous moment.

This is the thought that passed through their minds.

Did you ever stop and think that a true Yooper that loves the great outdoors spends his whole life working and collecting things so he can be successful on his hunting and fishing adventures, then when he goes to that perfect duck blind in the sky his wife has a yard sale trying to peddle his dreams.

This can be bad enough but in most cases his dreams are lucky to bring a nickel on the dollar he had spent for it. In fact, a lot of the things they have laying around are worthless to almost anyone but them. They may use them, or they may have plans to use them someday. The latter is the most likely reason they have it lying around. A normal hunter or fisherman has a garage full of "things" they just may need someday if Lady Luck should ever strike.

Of course if Lady Luck was to strike he would be in serious trouble because chances are he would never be able to find what he had been saving for thirty years waiting for just this moment in life.

119

So what happens, he rides into the sunset and the family starts cleaning out his things. During this time you will hear over and over, "I wonder why in the world dad ever kept this, it was never of any use from the day he got it." So all this goes into the garage sale box and his dreams are once again on the open market.

Then after the garage sale an even more devastating thing can take place. Here comes a truck with one of those big metal bens on it backing into his driveway. Off the truck this red box rolls, and then the kids get to throw all those valuable artifacts from dad's adventures through life into it. A dream hitting the bottom of a dumpster makes a rather hollow sound.

So Eino figured, dad of the great outdoors, have you ever stopped to think what you are worth? A good Saturday yard sale if it doesn't rain with the leftovers tossed into a dumpster.

In my travels as a game warden there is one thing that I saw over and over. This was the look on a child's face as they were with dad on an afternoon of adventure. It did not matter if they were fishing along a creek bank, walking through the woods with their bird dog, or just enjoying the fellowship of each other.

It also did not matter if they were rich or poor in the sight of others. It did not matter if they had the newest and best up to date clothes and equipment or just some hand-me-downs and yard sale specials. Money does not matter when dad and the kids are enjoying an afternoon together.

I can sit here more than fifty years later and recall some days of enjoyment with my dad like they were yesterday. The pictures are still in my mind from those adventures like they were playing on a high definition TV today. Needless to say all I have today are those memories about dad.

For this bond is the key to handing the love and respect for the great out-of-doors down to the next generation. As the old saying goes, "you can tell someone something and they may remember it, but you show them it and they will always remember it."

There is no doubt in this old game warden's mind that this is the key to getting the next generation involved in the out-of-doors. You can have all the programs, youth hunts, free fishing days, and they all help, but the key is to build that love for nature on those outdoor adventures with dad and mom.

I think there is no better testimony for parents when they reach the end of the trail to have their children sit around and recall all the adventures of years gone by. This is what has made our nation what it is, and this will keep it like it should be for the next generation.

The following men are just a couple of examples of what a husband and father should be and at the end I will tell you why.

Arvo

I want to tell you just what I feel is the reason our nation is as great as it is, and just who we have to be thankful to, that it was that way when we grew up.

Now when a person, society considers important passes away we have 24-7 coverage of just how great they were and all that they have contributed to our Nation. I personally feel there is a different reason our Nation has survived all the years it has and when we lose this we are all going to be in trouble.

This week a man passed away that will never make the history books. In fact, he will never be remembered for being a great inventor or statesman. No, he will only be remembered by those of us that knew him as a hard working, loving husband and father trying to raise his kids up right and support his family.

He grew up on a small U.P. farm and later went to work in the mines in the Crystal Falls area. He could speak two languages English and Finish. When the mines closed he transferred over to Manistique to work at Inland Quarry. He came to our town with his wife, three daughters, and one son. For those that knew him at Inland they all talked about his work ethics and how hard he worked and how strong he was. He loved the great outdoors and you could get him to talk about it whenever you stopped by to see him.

In fact the last time I was at his house with Wifee he asked all about camp and if the kids had been up there lately. He loved to come by camp. A true Yooper never gets tired of this. He asked about all our kids and how they were doing. His three girls were at his home now because time was short for dad, and his son was making plans to get home from his base in Texas. Wifee heard he would like one more of her lemon pies, so she made a couple and took them out for this family.

This past Sunday Arvo Kettula went off to join his wife of so many years. Arvo will never go down in history, but he left a legacy that all dads would be proud to leave behind, a family you can be proud of.

What makes out Nation great? It is the thousands and thousands of men just like Mr. Kettula who through the years have been the backbone of the United States of America. Those who when they pass on leave another generation of hard working offspring to carry on the family values they had.

What do I remember about Arvo? Telling Wifee, "Tell John to shoot them (the deer) in the neck and they drop right there and you don't have to look for them!"

Mr. Kettula sweets & Amy venison

You could take a man out of the mines, but not the mining stories out of the man.

Always Liked to greet people at church in Finish. He could speak two languages English and Finish.

Caught in bear trap while hunting as a young man.

As I have said so many times, "Life is made up of memories" and there are a lot of good ones here.

97 Years Strong

I want to take some time and talk about another one of the old timers I knew that went to that perfect deer blind in the sky in the past week. Of course he went at the age of 97 and was as sharp as a tack right up to the end. To me it is really something when someone up in the 90's can recall as plain as can be things that happened long before I was even born.

You have to think like Wifee and I to understand how much enjoyment we get just listening to all the tales some of these old timers have. Of course the other side of the equation is that a lot of them enjoy reliving some of the "good old days" too.

If a person was not as old as I am and had not grown up in the U.P. they could easily believe that just maybe the truth was being stretched a little. But I know from my dad and others, who were around during the same time period that life was really like we were told.

Last Fall we were out in Gulliver to visit Neely and he told us he would like to take a ride back into the area where his camp was and see the swinging bridge over the Manistique River once again. He told us he was going to drive back there by himself, but he had trouble reading the small number on the padlocks. He said they were logging off some of his son's property so he could get in, but if someone locked the cable he could not see well enough to get it open.

I told him that at 97 he did not need to be taking trips back to the "middle of no-where" by himself. So Wifee and I told him we would pick him up on the first of the week and all three of us would take a ride back into his old stomping grounds. What a great time we had.

Neely had lived on Townline Road before moving out to Gulliver Lake. So as we drove along he filled us in on what had happened as we passed certain areas. We went by one old apple orchard that sits back off the road and he told us that he had killed two monster bucks back in that orchard two years in a row. But then he said, "For some reason I just never went back there and hunted again."

He told us other areas where he had shot some nice bucks, but one of the things he was sure proud of was the successful hunter his wife was. They had been married almost 75 years and they had always did everything together.

In fact, I used to find their car parked up on the Highwater Truck Trial in the fall as they were back in the marshes looking for wild cranberries. They usually found them too, and even when they were up in age where most people would have given up going back in the marsh looking for them they still did.

Then in the spring I would find them out hitting the backwoods looking for morels. They would cover a lot of area trying to find just the right spot. I teased Neely right up to this spring about how he needed to get out there and look for some morels.

We drove down Rice Road and into both his boy's camps so he could check them out and came to the swinging bridge. Neely had to get out and walk across it just once more. It brought back so many memories of my dad who would just do something he had done a million times before, just because he wanted to.

Of course Wifee was not too impressed with a 97 year old Neely going out on the bridge, but he just laughed at her with that laugh he had. I took a couple of pictures of Wifee and Neely out on the bridge and then we went to the Dreamland Restaurant for lunch.

Wifee told me later that when I was up taking care of the bill Neely reached over and took her hand and said, "Thanks for taking this old man out for a ride and putting up listening to all his old stories." Of course Wifee told him we enjoyed it.

If you stop and think about it there are fewer and fewer of the "Old School" left to sit and listen to anymore. It seems that more and more are falling by the wayside, but it sure was my pleasure to get to know so many of them. Besides a lot of them like to tell the old Game Warden a story or two.

(I want to say that Neely was as sharp and witty in the last week of his life as he was all the years we knew him.)

The Key

If there is anything that makes me thankful that I took the time to do my books and spend time each week doing the Fish Report, it is some of the notes and letters I receive. One thing I have heard over and over is where a son has got so caught up in life that he somehow forgot about that old buddy of his back home.

#1, I received a note from a real successful teacher that said after hearing me tell stories at a banquet and reading my books that he had made it a point to set a weekend a month aside to just spend some time with dad. He said, "Just to maybe do nothing, but to take a ride through their old stomping grounds and let dad tell him once again those stories he used to enjoy."

#2, One week in the Fish Report I wrote about Neely and spending time with him and listening to his stories. I don't know if you are aware of the fact that the Fish Reports cover a lot of ground over the internet. When people read the story on Neely I received some real heart touching letters back.

One party wrote a two page letter telling about how lucky we all were with Neely because he was so sharp right up to the end. He told me his dad had a stroke later in life and when they were out at camp or driving around he would try to tell his tales about his adventures in the past, but had so much trouble trying to speak and tell them, he would give up and pull back into a shell. He told me they would try to make dad go ahead and tell the stories, but it never again was to be like it was for so many years that they had taken for granted.

He said now he would give anything to be able to sit with dad and just pay attention and listen to his tales once again. More than that he wished his kids could have spent more time with grandpa when he was able to relive life in his stories. But needless to say those days are gone forever.

#3, Another party dropped me a note after reading the article and said he could only think of his dad, and how he would give anything to be able to spend another week out at camp with him during hunting season. He said we always seem to take things for granted, never realizing that the hunting season will come when dad is not longer there to retell that same story for the hundredths time.

He said you laugh now with a tear in your eye, but back then you figured you could tell the story better than dad could because you had heard it so many times.

These two successful men, along with a number of other people, made it a point to contact and tell me how they wished they just had another week to spend like it used to be. So please don't take the time you have with your loved ones for granted because life can be awful short, then those times we can spend together are lost forever except in our memories.

In closing this chapter I am going to attach a letter I received from Iraq.

Dear Sgt. John A. Walker,

My name is Shawn Weisler. I just recently read one of your books, "Human Are Nuts!" for the first time. My local library sent it to me amongst a collection of others. You see I am currently deployed to Iraq right now. I am a Security Force (or Military Police) member of the US Air Force. Your book caught my eye and once I saw that you are a fellow Michiganer I had to read your book.

I was born and raised in Charlevoix County area. I grew up in Boyne City, MI. (if you are not familiar, I am about 45 minutes SW of the Mackinac Bridge.) So yes I am a TROLL. I consider myself part Upper because I went to college for a year at Michigan Tech in Houghton. Don't know if that counts or not.

After high school and attending college at MTU and then Grand Valley State down in Grand Rapids, I enlisted in the Air Force. I have been in the USAF for a little over two years. I have been stationed in South Korea for a year and then moved to Anchorage, Alaska and am stationed there now. I deployed from Alaska to Iraq back at the end of September.

So far the deployment is going really well. It can be very trying at times over here, especially spiritually. I must add that I am also a fellow believer in Jesus Christ. I trusted Him and asked Him to be my savior over two years ago now. The Lord's strength he gives me is what gets me through each day. Lots of prayers, reading His Word, and worship keep my spirits up. Lots of love from family and friends sent to me in packages, letters, & E-mails sure help too.

I like to read books, but good wholesome books are hard to come by. I want to say I truly enjoyed your book. I could relate to a lot of the stories written in your book. I found myself at times wishing my dad and I had as good of relationship as you and your sons have. I have already forgiven my father for things of the past and am prayfully moving slowly to build a better relationship with him. One thing that we do both like to do is hunt whitetail. I would of loved to of been out there with my Grandpa, Dad, and Uncle this year. My Uncle Randy shot an 8-point, a nice one I hear. He also shot at a bigger buck but only grazed it, no blood just hair.

I pray for my family members who are not saved. My father is one of them, to the best of my knowledge that is. I have tried to witness to him. Hunting season would have been a good opportunity to be a good testimony for my family. However, I did pray that the Lord would bless my family back home with a deer and He did, my uncle!

Your stories inspired me to strive to develop that same kind of legacy to pass on to my future children, if the Lord wills it for me to have children that is. I would love to someday take my boy fishing or hunting and teach him how to shoot and take my family camping and hiking.

The family atmosphere you have sounds a lot like families I see at the church I attend back in Alaska. (Independent Baptist Church of Anchorage) They have a great summer camp for kids, teens, and even a family camp. I love that church small and friendly atmosphere. I am looking forward to returning and seeing everyone again.

Well, that is about all I have to say, I wanted to thank you for your wonderful stories you have gathered and put into a book. Please keep up the writing; you are doing a fine job. I am sure you would have never of thought one of your books would of made it to another part of the world, all the way over here in Iraq! I enjoyed reading your book for it brought back a lot of memories of home. Helped my time go by quicker over here.

Sincerely, A Fellow Brother in Christ,

2nd note:

Thanks John;
Your books are great, my father read every page until his death in Nov. His favorite books was *Whatdaya Mean A Bad Attitude.* So I slip it in his casket so he had some good reading on his journey with God.

Thanks, God Bless, Jim

The little guys on the cover getting ready to go out hunting.

The side of the Conservation Officer you don't
see, spending a Saturday working with a group of youth.

You wonder how things have changed in the U.P.?
This is the house that my dad's parents started
their housekeeping together in.

I get ask all the time if I miss working as a conservation officer. My usual reply is that I was in at the tail end of the best times. I feel this way because of the attitudes on both sides of the fence.

Needless to say there have always been those that felt it was their worse nightmare to come across a game warden in their everyday activities. Even if they were doing nothing wrong, for the moment, they were not too happy when they figured that it was not good if the local game warden even knew the area where they operated.

I can recall one time when dad and I were back in the middle-of-nowhere and had given a couple of Conservation Department employees a ride back with us so they could check out a forest fire that had been burning there.

We had a means to get back there with the "bug" dad had made from an old Model-A, while the only way they could have gotten into this area was to walk.

As dad and the two men were talking a couple of deer ran through a large opening. Dad pulled up with his rifle, but seeing there was not a buck in the herd did not shoot.

Later on I ask dad about the fact he had already filled his tag, would he have shot another buck if there had been one running across the opening. He told me he probably would have and that the two Conservation Department employees would not have figured it was wrong because someone down the road at camp would have tagged it.

Back then you were not only hunting for the love of getting out there, but also to put some meat on the table during the winter months. Back then Thanksgiving dinner was usually a fresh venison roast, not a turkey you could not afford.

131

I think the tale below kind of tells you about how a lot of people feel things have changed.

How Was That Again?

I have written articles before about the fact that the tax payers are now paying for two of everything. It seems like the federal government is more and more encroaching on states rights in the area of hunting and fishing. We the tax payers are now paying for both state and federal law enforcement and when this happens someone has to pay the bills.

This being the case it is no wonder you are more and more reading about these organizations coming up with new ways to pay the bills. This past week I was reading an article where the U.S. Fish and Wildlife Service want to charge a $30 fee for trappers to trap in some of the federal refuges.

Could this be the start of something new? Could you not see where a trapper, hunter, and other user's of federal forest and other federal areas had to purchase a stamp like a duck stamp along with their state permits? Don't laugh because you have about a zillion professional bureaucrats that have nothing to do but figure out how to collect more money from people to pay for their programs, some of which should never have come to be in the first place.

I was sent something the other day that maybe better explains how we get took by government.

A cowboy was watching his herd in a remote backwoods pasture when suddenly a brand-new BMW advanced out of a dust cloud towards him. The driver, a young man in a Brioni suit, Gucci shoes, Ray Ban sunglasses and YSL tie, leans out the window and asks the cowboy, If I tell you exactly how many cows and calves you have in your herd, will you give me a calf?"

The cowboy looked at the man, obviously an Exspurt, then looked at his peacefully grazing herd and calmly answered, "Sure, Why not?"

The Exspurt parks his car, whips out his Dell notebook computer, connects it to his Cingular RAZR V3 cell phone, and surfs to a NASA page on the Internet, where he calls up a GPS satellite

132

navigation system to get an exact fix on his location which he then feeds to another NASA satellite that scans the area in an ultra-high-resolution photo.

The young man then opens the digital photo in Adobe Photoshop and exports it to an image processing facility in Hamburg, Germany. Within seconds, he receives an email on his Palm Pilot that the image has been processed and the data stored. He then accesses a MS-SQL database through an ODBC connected Excel spreadsheet with email on his Blackberry and, after a few minutes, receives a response.

Finally, he prints out a full-color, 150-page report on his hi-tech, miniaturized HP LaserJet printer and finally turns to the cowboy and says, "You have exactly 1,586 cows and calves."

"That's right. Well, I guess you can take one of my calves," says the Cowboy.

He watches the young man select one of the animals and looks on amused as the young man stuffs it into the trunk of his car. Then the cowboy says to the young man, "Hey, if I can tell you exactly what your business is, will you give me back my calf?"

The young man thinks about it for a second and then says, "Okay, why not?"

"You're a bureaucrat-exspurt for the U. S. Government", says the cowboy. "Wow! That's correct," says the Exspurt, "but how did you guess that?"

"No guessing required." answered the cowboy. "You showed up here even though nobody called you; you want to get paid for an answer I already knew, to a question I never asked. You tried to show me how much smarter than me you are; and you don't know a thing about cows."

"This is a herd of sheep; now give me back my dog."

Do you ever have the feeling you have met some people that would fit this little tale and the sad thing is they are running the show?

I have always felt that there were those out there I was trying to catch that could have qualified for a doctorate degree in poaching.

Now you have to understand that when a young person goes off to college there is this gray haired old guy that stands there and tells him all that he knows to qualify this youth to become an Exspurt. So is it really any different with a third or forth generation poacher?

Those that are trying to take over in the family practice will only succeed if they are willing to listen to those that have been doing it for years and know all the little twists to outwit the game warden.

Needless to say it is the same way on the other side of the fence. The one thing that is really missing now is the old school being around to give advice to the newer officers. Some things are not taught in books but passed on down the line from father to son.

I will be the first to admit that I cannot say I managed to catch every person I figured was up to no good out there. In fact there were a few of them that I never did catch no matter how many times I tried. The worse thing is even years after I retired they were never willing to tell me just how they managed to outwit me so many times.

I could sit for hours waiting for them to show up and when they did they were as clean as a whistle. I could try and catch them in different locations at different times of the day, no luck. I would try to back-track them to figure out just what they were up too, I always came to a dead end.

I used to tell people it is just like going out hunting or fishing, if you went out fishing and day after day limited out with no effort at all, pretty soon fishing would be no fun at all. In most outdoor activities it is the challenge that makes it so interesting and this is what keeps your interest.

But then to even things out in life there seems to be those that whenever they go out and manage to bend the rules a little or even a lot it seems there is a game warden waiting for them behind the next tree.

I have had cases where I was sitting out in the middle-of-nowhere catching up on some paper work (The part of the job that makes life so interesting but justifies all those jobs in the Big House.) when along comes a vehicle. Then would you believe it out the window comes a rifle barrel and pow! Someone takes a shot from the truck and there you sit.

So you pull up and here is a guy that has been caught dozens of times before. Some people just have no luck at all and if they did have any it would be bad luck all the time.

Then there is the guy that gets away with his poaching slick and clean. Nobody, especially the game warden, even knew he had done what he did. But! Human nature says for a lot of these poachers half the fun when you outwit the local game warden is you just have to brag about what you did.

There were cases where even if the local game warden knew something had taken place he had no idea who was even in the area when it happened. It was one of those times that the local rumor mill may have given him a clue that a deer had been poached but that was all he had, a rumor.

But would you believe it the poacher that was home, free and clear, got hoof and mouth disease in one of the local water holes with a visiting game warden sitting at the next table. In fact he not only told what he had did, he laid out every detail just how he had managed to outfox the local warden with the times, date, what he was driving, and even the gun he had used.

So then locked and loaded with all this information from the poacher himself the local warden drops in to see him. Now there is an art to talking to people and making them feel that you are a whole lot smarter than you really are. (In fact Lansing and Washington has this perfected.)

You sit down and tell him you want to ask him a few questions and just to be safe you are going to read him his rights before you even get started. Right off you make him feel like, he must know something because they usually only read people who are in trouble their rights. Right away he is on defense and you are on offence.

You then just happen to mention that you had heard that a deer had been shot out in a deer yard on Sunday afternoon. Then you lay out the time it took place, where the person parked that had shot it, the type vehicle they were driving, model, color, and even the license plate number, that you had written down walking into the house. (In his eyes you see a light come on that he seems to recognize some of these facts.)

Then you really make him wonder when you mention that from the information you have this deer was shot with such and such a rifle and that the shooter had two of his buddies (Jim and Joe) with him when he shot the deer. By now from the look on his face you see that his mind is outwitting his brain wondering just how I could know all these facts down to every detail never dreaming the reason is they came from his own mouth.

About then you take out a blank sheet of paper, and being the nice person you are, you even offer to let him use your ink pen to write in his own words just what took place that Sunday afternoon so he would not be accused of doing something he didn't do. Would you believe it, nine out of ten times they would give you their version of what happened.

You could then take his statement and call on Jim and Joe and they when seeing this statement would confess to what happened figuring, what's the use our buddy already squealed on us.

Then they would all get their day in court and always plead guilty seeing they were so sure somehow the game warden must have been there and saw what took place. They never dreamed they had really told on themselves in the coffee shop.

I never had a problem with those that actually did the poaching, but I did have other family members come up to me and blow their stack about the fact that it was totally unfair how I CAUGHT them. Somehow they felt I was suppose to catch them not have them catch themselves.

Winning a Blue Ribbon

In closing this chapter I guess what every game warden likes to hear is that after all his long cold nights, sitting out in the rain, freezing near to death so many times, is that even the poachers have a respect for how he does his job.

136

You that live in the asphalt jungle may not understand some of the backwoods way of life we up in the U.P. grew up with, but it has its own set of values. I have said while speaking at banquets that in a lot of cases those that are doing a little poaching may never invite the local game warden over for Sunday dinner, but they know when enforcing the law he is going to be fair.

I have always felt that if those living on the far side of the tracks were going to get a ticket for some activity, so was the local banker and his crew. Needless to say there were times when this could get an officer in trouble with the powers in the Big House.

It came to me one time through the grapevine that one of the better known poachers in the area where I worked told some of his buddies, "Walker takes all the fun out of violating, those other game wardens I could always figure out, but there is no rhyme or reason to the way he does things."

So not only do the game wardens have to try to keep one step ahead of the violators, he hopes that those out there breaking the rules have no idea where or when he may pop up.

Maybe this is the reason that long after I retired some of the locals sent me a copy of a couple of ballads they had written about me to sing at hunting camp.

Needless to say it was an interesting life.

1956 Conservation Officers class

As I have said over and over I would rather have it where whatever I was hunting walked right in and I got my shot before I ever had a chance to get nervous. Needless to say when you watch that nice buck work it's way into your shooting range for a half hour you are a wreck waiting to happen when he gets there. This is what nerves can do to a person and it does not really matter how good of a hunter he is.

Why Me Lord?

I have told the story where the bow hunter who was an excellent bow shot at targets would get so nervous when a deer walked in strange things would happen. Like the time he managed to release all his arrows between the tree stand he was sitting in and the deer standing broadside in perfect range.

In this case it was even more interesting, but the results were a little different too.

It seems that there was this bow hunter that would be the first to admit that just maybe he was not the best archer around. He had done his fair share of practice before the season began, but still there were some holes in his ability.

During the bow season he was way up north sitting in a blind that belonged to his brother-in-law. There were a number of deer working the area so it looked pretty promising. He had been sitting there for a little while when he all of a sudden realized a couple of deer had materialized from off to his right. He watched one nice one work its way into his shooting area.

He waited and waited and then let fly! Sure enough he missed and stuck his arrow a little to the right of the deer. He got another arrow ready, all the time getting more and more nervous. But he lets fly again and misses again. In fact, he went through all five of his arrows and about built a picket fence around the deer he was shooting at without so much as putting a scratch on it. Now he is out of arrows.

He figures he has nothing to lose so he gets out of his blind and walks out to where the deer is and collects all five of his arrows. All the time the deer is standing there watching him.

He goes back and gets in the blind and picks up his bow to try again. This time the law of average was on his side and he managed to put the arrow in the deer which he recovered a short time later.

Now why do some things like this happen, when at times deer can be so jumpy you cannot get ready to get a good shot at them, and other times they almost wait around until you hit them?

How often does an archer get 5-6 shots at a deer without it running off?

Cutting Down On The Odds

Then there are those, and at times I think there are more and more like these, who will do about anything to get a chance at a nice buck.

One time we were wandering around an area about five miles beyond the end of nowhere. We had heard that one of the local people who may have fudged once in a while had a deer blind back there near a creek.

After a lot of searching around we managed to find where he had built this blind. This blind was big enough to sleep in and in fact was built where you could stretch out and spend the night. He had a little one burner Colman stove to cook on and all the comforts of home. He had the whole inside of the blind covered with this spray on foam insulation for a two fold reason. First of all it would help to keep it warm inside and also it would cut down on the noise so chances of someone hearing you shoot at night were pretty slim. Needless to say he had gone through a lot of work packing all this stuff in here to make a blind this good.

A short ways out from the blind we also found where he had a bait pile where he had hooked up a motion light with wires running back to the blind. Inside the blind he had a couple of small batteries like you use on a garden tractor set up to power his motion light. Needless to say he was planning on cutting down on the odds of missing that buck that came in after dark. And from what our report was he had.

A New Touch to This Problem

Now as times keeps moving along there is always a new way to improve on an old method of poaching.

You take the poacher up above and add to the fact that now a lot of those trying to hunt after dark have installed a modern update. There have been cases now where they will build a blind and put out some bait and then install one of those small, solar yard lights that you can buy for just a few dollars from Harbor Freight.

These are the ones where you have the light with a little built in battery. Then they come with a little solar panel that you can put up in a tree to recharge the battery. They also have a motion sensor that will turn on the light if there is any movement at the bait pile. These lights are really something.

This was the case in one area and what made it all the worse was the fact that there was not any place where the game warden could hide close enough to grab the guy when he was using this poaching setup.

141

The local officer looked all over and could only come up with one method that just may work. When he got a tip that the party was not working for a couple of days he made plans to try and catch him.

He went out to the area of the blind with a walky-talky and set up to wait. On the first time out all he got was about froze while all the time his partner sat back in a warm patrol car drinking coffee.

The next night he went out again and got all set up. Sure enough right about dark he heard someone coming towards the blind. He watched them put out a little bait and then go and crawl into the blind. Now all he could do was wait and he dare not move for fear he would be heard.

In fact as time went along it got so cold he thought the poacher would hear his teeth chattering. But all he could do was wait.

A short time after dark sure enough the motion light came on and a couple of deer came into the bait. Nothing happened, other than he could tell that the poacher in the blind was watching them too.

Just a short time later he watched a nice buck come in from the right slowly moving into the glow of the light. As he watched the buck, he heard movement in the blind as someone opened the sliding window in the front of the blind.

He waited until the buck was standing broad side out at the bait pile in the glow of the solar, yard light. All of a sudden he saw a barrel of a rifle come out through the open window as the poacher was trying to get a shot at this nice buck.

Slowly our game warden reached up and grabbed hold of the barrel of the rifle and yanked it our through the blind window! It seems that the only place he could find where he could hide was under all the spruce trees he had dragged in to hide his blind. All the time he was only a couple of feet from our poacher on the other side of the wall of the blind.

In fact our poacher was so dumb founded he was still sitting there wondering what had happened to his rifle when the game warden stood up and placed him under arrest for night hunting.

Cabin Poaching

It seems like there is more and more of what is now commonly referred to as cabin poaching going on.

It is common for those of us that just enjoy seeing deer to have a food plot or a bait pile near camp so we can watch deer. The problem is that there seems to be a lot of those out there that have carried this too far.

In a lot of cases those that want to get a deer at any cost have placed motion lights over these food plots and bait piles so they can poach deer at night when they come in.

Now I have read way to many cases where violators were caught doing this. What scares you is having worked in the field I know for every poacher that does get caught there are always a dozen or more that never do.

Where has the idea of a "fair chase" to get a deer gone?

Author telling stories to school Kids in Wisconsin

Chapter 23

Conservation Officer's Stories **Upper Michigan Tales from a Game Warden's** **Perspective**

Some Strange Things Happen Out There

When you have spent as much time out in the woods as I have you can count on the fact that there will be some strange things happening that makes one stop and think.

Some of them seem to be letting you know things happen that are way beyond your control, while others make you just go aaaaw. More than once either my partner or I would look at each other and say, "Did you see that?" All the time knowing neither one of us really knew what it was we saw.

And NO! It wasn't "Big Foot!"

A Different Kind of Answer

If you have read any of my articles or books you know a lot about my outlook on life. There has never been any doubt in my mind that when you run into a problem you cannot handle there is only one thing to do, pray.

This was the case with a problem a friend of ours had. After our kids were all out of the nest we would borrow those of a couple that had been in our youth group at church. Of course they could well afford to lend us some because they had a dozen children running around their place.

Being a game warden and loving the outdoors like I do I did not have to twist their arms too hard to get them to go hunting or camping with me. Of course it was always fun to be able to run some stories by them to just watch their reaction.

Sitting out in the middle of the woods in a dark trailer you would be amazed at how serious some of their reactions could be when I told them stories about the sounds you hear

145

during the night. Needless to say Wifee and I had a great time whenever we got to take this crew out with us.

But that is not the story here. When the last one of this crew came along, she came along with a serious heart problem. She was such a little thing and to find out she had this serious condition made us all pray a little harder for her.

It finally came to the point that she was going to have to go down to the University of Michigan's hospital for heart surgery. This is always a serious operation, but on such a little thing it seemed all the more serious.

They had headed out for the U Of M hospital and I was out driving around praying as I did, for everything to work out for this little girl.

It was a cool, rainy evening with the rain coming and going. I was coming south on Thunder Lake Road, on my way home, when I came over a hill and a little ways down the road to a field where you could look across and see the home of this little girl and her family.

As I drove I was thinking of her, mom and dad, and the rest of the family and what they were going through. When I came to the opening I looked across the field at their house just as the sun was coming out as the rain was letting up.

Now this may seem hard to believe, but just as I looked at the house a bright rainbow showed up looking like it started at their home and arched across the sky.

Now you can believe this or not, but as I saw that rainbow I had a feeling like I had never experienced before, that everything was going to be all right for that little girl. It was just like the Lord wanted to let this old game warden know that he was looking out for her.

Everything did turn out all right, as I knew it would.

Having spent so many hours walking down 2-tracks or taking a trail through the woods I have often wondered, "What If?'

Too many times to count I have been walking and came across a large branch or stick that had fallen from a big dead tree and stuck in the 2-track you were walking on so hard you had to work to pull it out.

The "What If" part comes in when you stop and think what if someone had been walking down this path just when that stick came out of the tree with all that force. Needless to say it would ruin your day if it hit you.

The closest I have been to witnessing this actually take place was one day during the summer when Wifee and I, along with her brother and his wife, were driving around one Saturday morning. We had just turned a corner and started up a small hill when we saw this pickup coming down the hill towards us.

When this pickup was about a block from passing us a large section of an old dead tree broke off and came down at the pickup! This section of tree went right through the pickup's windshield. Half was now inside the truck with the rest sticking up through the window.

Needless to say, it was like, WOW! We stopped our vehicle and ran over to the pickup, where there was a young lady in it.

This large dead section of the tree had come through the windshield with such force that it had imbedded itself in the seat, floor, and over near the driver's side door. In fact, one section of the tree was right between the driver's legs.

How all these sections of wood had missed this young lady, who was the driver makes one wonder just who was watching over her on this Saturday morning. Someone had to be.

147

These were not little pieces of wood either but a large section of the old dead tree.

Of course, human nature has not really changed much because after the young lady was checked out and all the glass from the windshield was cleaned off her, her biggest worry was, "How am I ever going to explain to the owner of the truck what happened?" It seems it was someone else's truck she had just borrowed to run to town in.

And It Wasn't Big Foot Either

We will close this book with a few instances where you wish life had a rewind button.

Now, right off I want to say there was no way that this was 'Big Foot" or any relative of his! First of all they were running on all four, and second we got a good look, if only a quick one.

I say this because the same week I am putting this in this book, some "Big Foot" searchers are in the U.P. looking for him.

One day during bird season my partner and I were traveling down a 2-track along a sand ridge. It was a warm, sunny, fall morning just perfect for those that love the great outdoors.

All of a sudden "something" came out of the woods on my side of the 2-track and ran down the road in front of us for about 150 yards, and then cut back into the woods on the same side of the trail.

I looked at my partner, at the same time he was looking at me with both of us having a, "What was that" look on our face. Neither one of us had any idea what we had just seen it all happened so quick.

We got out and tried to find some tracks that could at least help us out trying to identify what it was, but there was not a track to be found in the loose, soft sand on the 2-track.

Now it was way bigger than a coyote and the color of a mountain lion, but did not appear to have a tail like they would have. It also seemed to have longer hair than something from the "cat" family would have.

What was it, we have no idea, but wouldn't it be nice if life had a rewind button on days when something like this happens because needless to say, you will probably never see it again.

Then there was the time we were up in the High Roll-A-Ways area. It was just before deer season and we were going through an area of second growth pine trees. Once again it was a nice, warm, sunny fall day only this time it was in the afternoon.

As we were driving down this 2-track we all of a sudden saw movement through the trees down the road in front of us off to the right. We saw flashes of dark brown and at first thought it was a deer because of the color and how tall it was.

Only what went across the 2-track in front of us wasn't a deer!

In fact, the only thing we could figure it was, was a large wolf. It was not the normal color you figure wolves should be, but what else would be this big? A coyote on steroids!

So you see there are some things that happen out there that we will never really understand or know the answers to, because "He" is not explaining them to us.

149

Conservation Officer's Stories
Upper Michigan Tales from a Game Warden's Perspective

Up here in the Great North Woods, there is a tendency to use terms or phrases to make a point. To some of you, they may be used in a way you never realized they could be. Other words or terms, you may just have not had the opportunity to ever use. This Backwoods Glossary is to help you out in understanding why we talk like we do.

U.P. (Upper Michigan): If, for some strange reason, you have never traveled in Michigan, these two letters would seem strange to you. First, understand that Michigan has two peninsulas the upper and lower. The Lower Peninsula is made up of two parts, Lower Michigan and Northern Michigan. But, the really important part of Michigan lies across the Mackinaw Bridge. This part of Michigan is called the U.P., for the Upper Peninsula of Michigan. The people up here in the U.P. live in their own little world and like it that way. The only problem is that most of the laws are passed down in Lower Michigan to correct their problems, and then they affect us, who may not even be part of that problem. Some of the Big City folks that pass these laws never have learned to understand and love the U.P. like we that live here do. The natives of the U.P. have trouble understanding the "why-for" about some of these laws; therefore they feel they really must not apply to them.

Two of the biggest industries in the U.P. are paper mills and the men that work in the woods supplying trees to these mills so they can produce their product. There are probably more colleges in the U.P., per capita, than anywhere else in the country. But even with this, there are still a lot of natives up here that feel you could sure ruin a good person if you sent them to one of these colleges. News of a serious crime will travel from one side of the U.P. to the other like a wild fire. Because most people up here are not used to it. To them, serious crimes are when someone takes a deer or some fish illegally and is dumb enough to get caught. They don't even take these crimes to seriously unless the poacher should step over the line and get to greedy.

Sports teams that play teams from other towns in the U.P. always seem to have relatives, or friends, on the other team. Everyone knows someone, or someone that married someone, that knew someone from over there. To win a state championship, you have to beat those teams from "down state". To do this is a dream come true for any red-blooded U.P. boy or girl.

When I was growing up, we had only had part-time radios. So we had to be Green Bay (Wisconsin) Packer and Milwaukee Brave fans. As a boy living in the Western U.P., we could not pick up any radio stations that carried broadcast of the teams from Lower Michigan. For this reason, we grew up feeling that we were a state unto ourselves. We could not be part of Lower Michigan, because it was just too far away, and the only way to get there was by boat. We knew we were not part of Wisconsin, so we were just the Good Old U.P.

Up here in the U.P., where life is tough, but things are good, and it is just a great place to live.

Some Backwoods (U.P.) Terms:

2-TRACK :(roads) The U.P. has hundreds of miles of this type of roads. All these roads consist of are two tire ruts worn into the ground from all the vehicle travel throughout the years. Usually you have a high, grass-covered center and mud holes in the low spots. This is one of the reasons that so many people in the U.P. feel you cannot live without a 4x4 pickup. These roads are never worked on or improved and you get what you see.

Blacktop Roads: These are the 2-tracks, which are worse than unimproved roads. They are covered by mud or clay and it is a real trick to stay between the trees on some of these. There are also a lot of these type roads for which the U.P. is famous. Many a fishermen or hunter has spent hours and hours trying to get out of one of these blacktop roads, usually after you misjudged what you were getting into. Two of the first things I learned after becoming a Game Warden stationed in the U.P. were: It's hard to get 2-ton stuck at fifty miles an hour, so wind it up and keep moving. The other one follows point one, you are never really stuck till you stop. In other words, if one of these blacktop areas sneaks up on you, floor it and don't stop 'til you reach high ground or hit something unmovable.

151

Poachers: These are not people that cook eggs in hot water, but may get themselves in hot water now and then. They are outlaws that rob the honest hunters and fishermen of their chance to get game and fish legally. In years past, it was a way of life in the U.P. that was passed down from generation to generation. When it was an accepted thing to do, the Game Warden not only had a hard time catching the poachers, but he usually had an even harder time trying to get a conviction in the local courts.

Shining: (Shinning, Shining, Shiners), Shiners are the poachers that use a spotlight to look for deer at night, in order to shoot them. Until the fines got to high, it was the way that a lot of the outlaws did their hunting here in the U.P. They would take a pair of spotlights, hook them up in their vehicle, and then drive around while casting the rays of the spotlights out into fields or an old orchard, until they spotted a deer. The deer, blinded by the bright light, would stand there staring at the light while the poacher got out his gun and shot it. There is really no sport in it, because it is so deadly. You will notice I spelled shinning, with two "n's" at times. Well, I did this on my tickets for dozens of cases throughout the years; until a State Trooper told me it was spelled wrong. He said it should only have one "n", so on the next couple tickets I changed how I spelled shining. You see for years, when I caught someone hunting deer at night with a spotlight, the only thing I would write for a charge on the ticket was the one word "shinning". With the one word spelled, Shinning, they knew what they did, I knew what they had done, and most important the average U.P. Judge knew what they were standing before him for doing. Well, the first time I caught a crew out spotlighting for deer and put shining (with one n) on their ticket they pled "Not Guilty". The spelling must have confused them and so was I.

Spearers: These are people that have a way of taking fish with the use of a spear. The spear can have from three to five prongs, with pointed tips; these prongs have barbs on the end to hold the fish on the spear after they spear it. Now in some areas, it is legal to spear certain types of non-game fish. The problem the Game Warden has is with those that spear trout, salmon, walleye, etc. or "game fish". When these fish come into real shallow water to spawn, a Game Warden will spend hour after hour watching the fish spawning in these areas.

Extractors: This is a term for those illegal fishermen that may come along a creek with a spear trying to extract the spawning fish from the creek. They may use other devices besides a spear. For instance, a weighted hook, hand nets, their hands, etc.

Gill Netters: These are people, both legal and illegal, that use a gill net to take fish. In some areas, there is a commercial fishery allowed with the use of gill nets, but in Michigan it is never legal for "sport" fishermen to use a gill net to take fish. A gill net is made up of nylon string in little squares (it looks something like a small woven wire fence) built so the fish will swim into the net putting their head through the square openings. Then, they get caught when their larger body will not fit through the squares and their gills keep them from backing out of the nets. I have observed illegal gill net fishermen take hundreds of pounds of steelhead in a couple of hours, if they set their gill nets in the right spot.

Fish house or fish shed: In areas of the U.P., along the great lakes where there is a legal commercial fishery, most of those businesses involved have a building where they clean, box in ice, and store their catch. They may also repair their nets in this building. On account of the smell around a full time commercial fishing operation, most of these sheds are located away from any residence. They also may be on the riverbank where the commercial fisherman ties up his fish tug. For this reason they are often used for illegal activity, sometimes by others than those that own them.

Deer camp: A deer camp can be any type of building used for offering protection from the elements. It is also used as a "get-a-way from home during the hunting season. Some are as nice as any house, better than some, while others may be made out of plastic, heavy paper, scrap lumber, or anything to keep the weather out. The following rules are some of the usual type that are proper for deer camp life.

(1) You cannot shave or take a bath, no matter how many days you may be staying at camp. You are allowed to wash your face and hands. But this is your own choice; you do not have to if you do not want to. This is one reason young boys love to go to deer camp with Dad.

(2) There is no proper way to dress while at deer camp, if it feels good wear it! You can even wear the same clothes all week long. This includes your socks, if you can catch them after the first three

153

days at camp.

(3) The "menu" is always made up of all the "proper" things that you cannot afford to eat all the rest of the year at home. Both good and bad for you.

(4) It is never wrong to tell a "true" story on another camp member. Remembering it is of more value if you can dress it up a little to make him suffer all the time you are telling it. During the telling of his misfortune we must all remember that we will all pay for our mistakes, sooner or later, if and when our hunting "buddies" find out about them.

(5) It is a crime, punishable by banishment, to talk about school, or schoolwork, or any work for that matter while at deer camp.

(6) You can throw, hang or just leave your socks and clothes anywhere they land when you remove them. You can hang your wet socks on anything that has something to hang them from to try and dry them out before the next days hunt. Always remembering it is "most" important to have dry socks by daybreak the next morning.

(7) What may be called work at home is not work at deer camp. Therefore getting things done at deer camp is not classified as work, but a team effort. For this reason, it is not wrong for a boy to do dishes, sweep a floor, pick up trash (that he missed getting in the trash can when he threw it that way, with one of his famous hook shots), or even do what Dad asks him to do, the first time Dad asks him to do it.

You would have to spend a week at a real U.P. deer camp to really know the true feeling of being a U.P. deer hunter. With these easy-to-apply rules, you can see why deer camp life is so important to a boy during his informative teenage years. It is really important that a young man start out with a proper perspective on life.

Big House: This is the Michigan State Capital; from some areas of the U.P. it can be over 400 miles away. In Lansing, this is where "they" compile all the rules and ideas that are put out to confuse the average hunter or fisherman, while out in the field. It is the feeling of a lot of U.P. sportsmen, that most of those that work down there, in Lansing's Big House, never in their lives set foot in the real out-of-doors, or wet a fishing line in a back woods stream. What they know, they got from someone that wrote a book without ever having set their feet in a real woods, or having gone backwoods fishing either. It is just passed on from desk to desk, year after year, put into volumes of rules and law books that we out in the field have to learn to live with. This while trying to enjoy ourselves out in the real Northwood's, Michigan's U.P.

Wifee: (W-IF-EE; wify) this is one's wife. To pronounce it right, you say the "W" sound, then the "IF", than draw out the "EE".

Big Lake: This can be any of the Great Lakes that border Michigan. Instead of saying, " I went fishing out on Lake Michigan Saturday". A native from the U.P. would say, "I went fishing on the Big Lake Saturday afternoon".

Off-road vehicles: ATV'S, ORV'S, dirt bikes, etc. These may be any of the type vehicles that are made primarily to operate off an improved road. Some may be homemade, while dealers sell others. In the U.P. you will find a lot of these used by sportsmen to get around when hunting and fishing.

Game Wardens: Conservation Officer, C.O.'s, and Game Wardens are all one and the same, up here in the U.P. They have been around for better than 100 years serving the people of Michigan. The stories they can tell and those told on them are told over and over around the U.P. This is how my newspaper, story telling got started.

Holiday Stations: Holiday? Here, in Michigan's U.P., you always hear the expression, "I'm going to stop by Holiday on the way". Some of you folks may not understand what a Holiday is and how far advanced the U.P. is over other areas of our country. I'll try to explain. Holiday; here in the North Country is a gas station-store. The Holiday Stations have been around for years and years, and in the U.P. they are like a mini-mall. The U.P. and Holiday were way ahead of the rest of the world on this idea of doing all your shopping in one stop. Get your gas plus whatever else you may need here at the Holiday. Sometimes it just takes awhile for you all to catch up to us, Yoopers.

Years ago when Christmas time came around, you went down to the Holiday. Here you did all your Christmas shopping. It had a great toy selection, in fact, in most U.P. towns the best to be found. If company dropped in for a surprise visit and you needed food items, off you went to the Holiday to get what you needed. When hunting and fishing season rolled around, they put out a paper and sales ad to get you into the Holiday to fill your needs, everything from guns and ammo, to poles, hooks, and line. If you snagged your waders, off you went to the Holiday for new ones. If your feet got cold out deer hunting, off to the Holiday for warm footgear you went. If your motorized deer blind broke down on a weekend, off to the auto parts section of the Holiday to get what you needed. What am I saying? Before the rest of the world was smart enough to think about putting other than gas and oil supplies in their gas stations the Holiday was there. Now they have moved up one more step because most Holiday Stations have copies of my books for sale.

Remember when traveling through the U.P., if a town does not have a Holiday station, keep on trucking till you find one because that town you are in has not arrived yet!

Copper Country: In so many parts of my book, you will read about things that took place in the Copper Country. This area covers what is called the Keweenaw Peninsula over to the area of the copper mines to the west. Those of us that lived in the Copper Country felt you were going into the world of the great unknown if you left Ontonagon, Houghton, Baraga, or Keweenaw County. In fact, a person growing up when I did may have left the Copper Country for the first time when he went into the service. The Copper Country is really a melting pot of people from all over the world. When I was growing up, it was nothing for some of the old folks not being able to speak English; they talked in their native language. In fact, one of the things that really bugged a teenage boy from the Copper Country was when there were a couple of girls your buddy and you wanted to get to know, and they would talk back and forth in Finnish, and we did not have the foggiest idea what they were saying. The history of the Copper Country is both interesting and unreal if you study it. A person could move away and be gone for years, but when asked where they are from, they always answer the Copper Country.

In the Copper Country, everybody knows somebody that knows somebody else. When on a radio show talking about my first book, "_A Deer Gets Revenge_", a party called in and wanted to know if I was Harry Theiler's grandson. Then another party called in and wanted to know if I was Tim Walker's brother. (Tim is my brother

156

that lives in a home in Hancock, MI, in the Copper Country). Copper Country people are special people that help make up a place called the U.P. where people know and care about each other. Come visit the U.P. and Copper Country someday, and you will see what I mean.

The other day: I keep telling my kids and the readers of my newspaper article that when I use the saying, "The other day", it could mean anytime between birth and death. It is up to the person you are talking too, to try and figure out what era you are talking about. Up here in the U.P., a party could start to tell you a hunting story by saying, " *The other day a buddy and I....*" and the story may have taken place back in the forties. (1940's) You have to remember that good stories never really get old; they just get better and added to in the telling of them. There was one officer I worked with could he tell stories! He would get going into a story and you would sit there and listen. Pretty soon bits and pieces would start to ring a bell. Then all of a sudden it would dawn on you that you were with him when "his story" took place, but you really never remembered it happening like he was telling it, or could it have? One of my boys called me from college a while back (another one of those times that means nothing in U.P. phrases) to ask me about the history of the 60's. This was for a paper he had to do for a history course. I told him, "Son, the 60's do not qualify as history yet. That is when your dad says, you know the other day, or awhile back, and that makes it today not history."

Exspurt: Sometimes in the U.P. we have our own way of spelling and understanding things. Here is one of those terms. I have a buddy that is a U.P. potato farmer. (You have to really wonder about anybody that tries to farm in the U.P.) But this buddy has a great definition for all those exspurts that rule down in the Big House. It is one of those terms you have to think about, but the more you think about it, the more you feel that this potato farmer may go down in history as a great U.P. philosopher. We will get talking about all those rules and laws the exspurts down in Lansing and Washington pass that are totally unreal, and my buddy will say, "Always remember that an ex-spurt is only a drip under pressure!" Now, I wonder.....

But then, you have all these TV shows on with an outdoor Exspurt on just about everything. Let's be real now. Do they ever get skunked out there fishing? Do you ever see them spending all day baiting hooks for the kids and getting the kids' lines untangled? Or get the boat unloaded and the motor won't start? Somehow, someway, I get the feeling these exspurts have never hunted or fished out there in the real world.

Let me give you an example of an Exspurt. One night I happened to be going through the cable channels and came across this Exspurt fisherman who had his own TV show. It happened that on this show he was fishing an area off Lake Superior that I was in charge of, so I decided to watch this show. Here is our Exspurt telling people how it should be done and where the nice steelhead fishing is in the U.P. As I watched, I couldn't believe it. So I got on the phone and called a Conservation Officer that worked for me and worked the area in the program. I told him, "John, you blew it and missed one. "He replied, "You must be watching the same program I'm watching." Then we both had a good laugh. Why? Because here was this Exspurt going along a trout stream running out of Lake Superior with an illegal device used to take trout in the spring of the year in that area! I told John, "Maybe we ought to send him a ticket in the mail. We have what he's doing on film, and he is even telling us he's doing it. "But you have to understand that this fishing Exspurt was a "troll"(a person that lives below the Big Mac Bridge.), and therefore, you get what you pay for. Now, remember what an Exspurt is, "A drip under pressure", and life will be a lot easier to understand.

Huskavarina edumacation; There has always been a feeling that there is more wisdom learned at the back end of a chain saw than you learn in college. The more some of us see and hear what is going on in our country, the more we have to wonder. It was always an amazement to those that worked out in the field for the government to see someone go off to the "Big House" on a promotion and forget everything they learned out in the field in the first six-months they were there! In fact, some of us always felt that about halfway down through the lower peninsula there was an invisible force field that made up a brain sucking machine, and by the time they passed through this going to the "Big House", they were useless to us living in the U.P.

We used to suggest that everyone after about a year or two down in Lansing's or Washington's "Big House" ought to have to spend six months back in the woods on the working end of a chain saw to get the feeling for how the real world lives again. That is why the U.P. is a special place, because from the woods, to the mines, to the papers mills, most of its people have a Husavarina Edumacation.

Sometimes I think it makes them special people as you can see by some of my stories.

Bugs: Back when I was a kid, a bug was not an insect. It was something you rode in going hunting. (Look at the picture in the books of us hunting in the 40's and 50's, and you will see our Bug.) You would take an old Model T or A and put oversize tires on it to raise it up off the ground. Then you would find some old tire chains. Most of the time they had no body left on them, and you were to hang on for dear life when you came to a big mud hole. A party always had this saying, "It's hard to get two-tons stuck at fifty miles an hour, but when you do you are really stuck." I always said, "You are never stuck till you stop, so the key is never to stop till you hit high ground again." All the hunters used these vehicles back before anyone ever heard of a 4x4 pickup. They were homemade, and you were really someone when you had one. In fact I cannot count the times we gave the Game Warden a ride back into the backcountry when he had something to check on because he was not lucky enough to own a "Bug". But, now if a person was to make one and try to use it, they would end up having to hire a secretary to file the nine thousand-four hundred-seventy-five million tickets you would receive for having this dangerous vehicle back in the woods. Man, those were the good old days; No ORV laws, no snowmobile laws, about half the hunting laws, and no Big Mac bridge to let all those idealists across into God's country.

Yoopers: Have you ever been asked, "What's a Yooper?" It seems that there are certain terms that the real world has not used yet. If you take the Upper Peninsula of Michigan abbreviated, namely "The U.P. and sound it out what do you get? It has to be the word Yooper. Therefore all the good people (natives only) that make their homes in the U.P. of Michigan have to be Yooper. Right?

Up here in Yooper Country we have our own jokes, our own Yooper singing groups, our own terms, and a great life style.

The one thing that you want to remember is that you are born a True Yooper. It cannot be bought, you cannot get it by living here for years and years, and you must be born a Yooper. We have a real problem with Trolls (Those that live below the Big Mac Bridge.) coming up to Yooper land then trying to act like or become one of us, it just cannot be done! You either have it or you don't. You can come see us, we are glad when you spend your money here, we like you for a friend, but remember when you leave Yooper Land you leave as you came, not as a Yooper.

Order Form

Order Form: *"Tales From A Game Warden"* Books
There are seven other books in the series. More than 80,000 copies of these books have been sold and more than $60,000 has been raised for the scholarship fund from the sale of these books.
1. A Deer Gets Revenge: ISBN 0-9639798-0-9
2. A Bucket of Bones: ISBN 0-9639798-1-7
3. Land of Big Fish: ISBN 0-9639798-2-5
4. Luck, Skill, Stupidity: ISBN 0-9639798-3-3
5. Humans Are Nuts: ISBN 0-9639798-4-1
6. But Honey! It Wasn't My Fault! ISBN 0-9639798-6-8
7. Whatdaya Mean! A Bad Attitude? ISBN 0-9639798-7-6
8. The Old School: ISBN 0-9639798-8-4 (This book by itself $12.50, plus $2.50 shipping & handling

Order from: JAW'S Publication, 530 Alger Ave. Manistique, MI 49854. Phone number: 906-341-2082 or E-mail: jawspub@charter.net. A single copy of the first 7 books is $10.00 plus $2.50 shipping & handling

A complete set of all 8 books is $62.50 which includes shipping.